"But where he met the individual man,

He show'd himself as kind as mortal can."

—BYRON, *Don Juan*

WILLIAM EDWARD WEST
1788-1857
KENTUCKY PAINTER

BY ESTILL CURTIS PENNINGTON

Lauren Rogers Museum of Art, Laurel, Mississippi

Published by the

NATIONAL PORTRAIT GALLERY

SMITHSONIAN INSTITUTION

City of Washington

1985

This catalogue and the exhibition have been made possible in part by generous support from the Chisholm Foundation, the Eastman Memorial Foundation, the Mississippi Arts Commission, the W. R. Stamler Corporation in Millersburg, Kentucky, and the Lauren Rogers Museum of Art in Laurel, Mississippi.

EXHIBITION ITINERARY

NATIONAL PORTRAIT GALLERY, Smithsonian Institution, Washington, D.C.
    April 12–June 16, 1985

LAUREN ROGERS MUSEUM OF ART, Laurel, Mississippi
    July 7–September 11, 1985

J. B. SPEED ART MUSEUM, Louisville, Kentucky
    September 27–December 9, 1985

LIBRARY OF CONGRESS CATALOG CARD NUMBER 85-60728

Cover:
ROBERT EDWARD LEE
Oil on canvas, 76.2 x 63.5 cm. (30 x 25 in.) , March 1838
Washington and Lee University, Lexington, Virginia
Catalogue number 31

The couplet on the half-title page is from Canto 8: 64 of *Don Juan* by George Noel Gordon, Lord Byron.

Frontispiece:
THE MUSES OF PAINTING, POETRY, AND MUSIC
Oil on canvas, 95.9 x 83.2 cm. (37¾ x 32¾ in.) , 1825
Corcoran Gallery of Art, Washington, D.C.
Catalogue number 19

Contents

v

Foreword

"Mysterious tides move within the direction of attention," wrote Edgar P. Richardson at the beginning of his pioneering book, *Painting In America*. Richardson was referring to the shifting interests of artists, from one generation to another, but his observation might equally well be applied to those who chronicle the lives of artists.

When Richardson wrote *Painting In America* in 1956, he characterized the Kentucky painter William Edward West as having "a fine, fresh, youthful, romantic talent." But he went on to say that "too little of his work is known to show whether that youthful promise was all, or whether an interesting and significant talent is hidden here." Here, indeed, is a lapse in the "direction of attention," since West was surely one of the more fascinating and talented American artists of the 1820s and 1830s, yet he had dropped into almost total obscurity by the 1950s. Now, at last, Estill Pennington has taken the first steps towards placing West more securely in the history of American art, and we are grateful to him for sharing his energy and enthusiasm with us, and for writing a new chapter in the chronicle of American portraiture.

West must have enjoyed his life at least as much as his art. He emerges from Mr. Pennington's account as a sociable and entertaining man, alert to new experiences and ready to take advantage of every opportunity that might lead to the advancement of his career. He was fortunate in his friends and acquaintances. In Baltimore he was introduced to a young military man, just promoted to lieutenant, and persuaded him to have his best uniform sent up for a sitting. Thus West recorded Robert E. Lee at the beginning of his notable career. When he went abroad, he carried an introduction to Washington Irving, then in a diplomatic post, and through Irving not only met a number of prospective sitters but was (apparently) given some confidential diplomatic assignments. In Italy he accepted a commission to paint a portrait of Lord Byron, and the sitting provided West with both a notable portrait (which helped to make his reputation) and with anecdotes for the diversion of scores of acquaintances.

Dr. Richardson, as one of the early Commissioners of the National Portrait Gallery, helped to formulate its mission, which has included the exploration of portrait artists whose lives and work have been, as he put it, "imperfectly explored." As the founder of the Archives of American Art, Dr. Richardson established a center for the collection of original and microfilmed documents about American artists, and encouraged scholars to use these documents, and to add to them. Today, both the National Portrait Gallery and the Archives of American Art are part of the Smithsonian Institution, and the author of this book provides another happy conjunction of these two bureaus in his work. Mr. Pennington was a member of the staff of the Archives of American Art when he revived his interest in West; and, when he saw that his research had turned up enough information to produce a satisfactory biography, and enough portraits to comprise a revealing exhibition, he approached the National Portrait Gallery to see if it would be interested. The present book, and the exhibition it accompanies, are the result. When Mr. Pennington was appointed director of the Lauren Rogers Museum of Art in Mississippi it became possible to share the exhibition, not only with the Lauren Rogers but also with the J. B. Speed Art Museum in West's native Kentucky. We are deeply grateful to the lenders to the exhibition for parting with their works for the extended period these three locations demand, and for all those who have shared information and documents with Mr. Pennington so that he could bring to life once again this refreshingly skilled artist.

ALAN FERN

Director,
National Portrait Gallery

Lenders to the Exhibition

THE ART COLLECTION, Tulane University, New Orleans, Louisiana
THE BALTIMORE MUSEUM OF ART, Baltimore, Maryland
PERCIVAL T. BEACROFT, JR., Rosemont Plantation, Woodville, Mississippi
BOSTON PUBLIC LIBRARY, Boston, Massachusetts
THE CIRCUIT COURT FOR BALTIMORE CITY, Baltimore, Maryland
MRS. GAILLARD CONNER AND MRS. MARY C. STEIN
CINCINNATI HISTORICAL SOCIETY, Cincinnati, Ohio
CORCORAN GALLERY OF ART, Washington, D.C.
H. RICHARD DIETRICH, JR.
JOHN PAGE ELLIOTT
WILLIAM BARROW FLOYD
THE HOUGHTELING FAMILY
GERTRUDE MCNABB MEISSNER
MIAMI UNIVERSITY ART MUSEUM, Oxford, Ohio
STATE HISTORICAL MUSEUM, Mississippi Department of Archives and History,
        Jackson, Mississippi
MUNSON-WILLIAMS-PROCTOR INSTITUTE, Utica, New York
THE MARYLAND HISTORICAL SOCIETY, Baltimore, Maryland
NATIONAL PORTRAIT GALLERY, Edinburgh, Scotland
NATIONAL PORTRAIT GALLERY, Smithsonian Institution, Washington, D.C.
THE NEW-YORK HISTORICAL SOCIETY, New York, New York
POYDRAS HOME, New Orleans, Louisiana
CAROLINE SHIELDS SESSIONS
THE J. B. SPEED ART MUSEUM, Louisville, Kentucky
TENNESSEE STATE MUSEUM, Tennessee Historical Society Collection, Nashville, Tennessee
THE UNIVERSITY OF DELAWARE, Newark, Delaware
THE UNIVERSITY OF KENTUCKY ART MUSEUM, Lexington, Kentucky
UNIVERSITY OF VIRGINIA LIBRARY, Manuscripts Department, Charlottesville, Virginia
NELL FOSTER WALTZ
WASHINGTON AND LEE UNIVERSITY, Lexington, Virginia

Author's Preface

with Some Explanations

*"This gentleman is one of those able artists who do honour
to our country, and raise its reputation for talent and
virtue in Europe; yet I have very imperfect information
respecting him."*

William Dunlap, *A History of the Rise and Progress of the
Arts of Design in the United States,* 1834

The rise-to-fame-and-decline-into-obscurity scenario is predictable enough for any artist. Perhaps no less predictable is the rescue effort, complete with color transparencies, rediscovered works of art retrieved from dusty storage bins, and crumbling, yellowed letters with one phrase that sets the entire story right. In the case of William Edward West, the "imperfect information" had not been perfected since Dunlap's day, and provided for me the essential challenge.

I first learned of William Edward West, "the celebrated Kentucky painter who travelled to Europe and painted Lord Byron," in a lecture given by Mrs. Edna Talbott Whitley (1891-1984) in 1956 at my grade school in rural Kentucky. Mrs. Whitley wrote a marvelous book on antebellum Kentucky portraiture, which is still the definitive study of that fine tradition. Twenty-five years later, when I began my research, I called upon Mrs. Whitley, and she told me stories of the West brothers and their trips down the Mississippi River by flatboat to New Orleans.

When I was a student at the George Washington University, Linda Neumaier of the Catalog of American Portraits in the National Portrait Gallery showed me a photograph of a painting of Robert E. Lee as a young man, by West. I thought it one of the finest nineteenth-century portraits I had seen. The quest for West was on!

While working for the Archives of American Art as an area specialist, charged with finding the papers of artists, I renewed my own Kentucky heritage by searching for the papers of West, Oliver Frazer, Joseph Henry Bush, and others. The West research quickly became the most fascinating and absorbing, for two reasons: he seemed to have traveled so extensively as to have been on the scene of almost every important event before the War Between the States, and I was attracted to his very romantic style of painting. Yet, when I began to seek out documents and examples of his work, very little readily emerged.

The search for the West papers became an obsession with me, and I visited all the principal sites in America where he had lived and worked. In Philadelphia, Baltimore, Nashville, Cincinnati, Lexington, New York, and New Orleans, bits and pieces and many works of art began to appear, but still very little primary evidence. Then, in the curatorial files of the Corcoran Gallery of Art, which had been given *The Muses* by a descendant, I discovered a photocopy of an old article on West in *Putnam's Monthly* magazine with an appended note that "letters and manuscripts are owned by his great-niece, Mrs. Charles E. McNabb." Her last address, dated 1958, was in Bethesda, Maryland, but in 1981 there was no mention of her in the telephone directory, and I could find neither Mrs. McNabb, nor her descendants, nor the papers.

While I was pondering the problem at my desk at the Archives, the telephone rang, and an attorney from Nashville, Tennessee, was on the line about a portrait of West's father—the silversmith and inventor, Edward West, Jr. He had heard of my work from Charles Pittenger of the Kentucky Historical Society, with whom I had had many conversations concerning West. A trip to Nashville to see the portrait was rewarded with a copy of the West family genealogy. Poring through the descendants of Edward West, Jr., I came upon Mrs. McNabb, and discovered that she had a daughter, Gertrude Meissner. I managed to find Mrs. Meissner and the West papers in Barnesville, Maryland, some twenty-five miles from where I lived, after searching all over the country!

The discovery of the West papers filled enough gaps in his life and times so that I could begin to plan a catalogue and an exhibition. The papers contained not only a critical letter from Natchez, Mississippi, identifying the time and place of his tenure there; they also included a complete list of all correspondents and associates, as well as copies of letters to West, and his own handwritten account of the Byron sitting. His last letters were there, too, giving a brief, sad glimpse into the artist's final days.

Two aspects of the nineteenth century, the great upheaval which we call the Civil War, and the overly protective morality of the discreet Victorians, interfered with a complete understanding of the artist's life. An account that I discovered in the Tennessee State Library in Nashville disclosed the information that, at the time Federal troops were occupying Nashville after the war, a music store owned by John B. West, William E.'s brother, had been sacked, and a great many of West's papers which were stored there lost. His book of drawings, really an inventory of his sitters, had been sold at auction for fifty dollars after his death, and remains unlocated. Finally, his papers had been censored by his family and heirs for two reasons important to them: a fear of scandal resulting from West's ambiguous attachment to Felicia Hemans, a married woman; and the embarrassment of his bankruptcy while abroad. I can understand and respect the family feeling on these two very personal matters, although I suspect that a great deal of information was lost in the process.

The last person to really see the West archives intact was Nellie Porterfield Dunn. Mrs. Dunn's father had bought several of West's paintings at the estate auction. She was from Nashville, and knew the family and had complete access to what remained of his things for her article in *Putnam's*. Because she was in touch with the oral tradition surrounding West, as conveyed by descendants who knew him, and because she had access to the papers in their undisturbed state, I believe that she really knew more of him than I have subsequently come to know. But this only provokes in me a kind of nostalgia for the manners and customs of the Old South, and I do not regret my discovery that one closed door has remained between myself and a full knowledge of West's life.

There is one element in the research of this artist which is elusive and hard to define: the oral tradition of the South. As Southerners can be preoccupied with genealogy, it is often very difficult to get them to focus upon anything other than their innumerable cousins. There is an advantage to that obsession when one is working on a portraitist. The event of the sitting is likely to have created a resonance in subsequent generations, usually highly embroidered but with some elements of truth intact. Thus, Mrs. Whitley had heard stories about the West brothers from the second generation of Abram Spears's family, and, as she was rather scrupulous about her facts, information was conveyed by the non-empirical mode: word of mouth. Genealogy is no less important than the oral tradition. I found the West papers through a genealogical search, and a deeper acquaintance with each sitter provided a richer context for West, himself greatly infatuated with large families like his own, and their doings.

There are several important sources and individuals whom I wish to acknowledge. William Edward West was far from unknown in his own time, and the accounts of him which appear in William Dunlap's *A History of the Rise and Progress of the Arts of Design in the United States* and Henry Tuckerman's *Book of the Artists* give an indication of the esteem in which he was held by his contemporaries. Nellie Porterfield Dunn's article "An Artist of the Past: William Edward West and His Friends at Home and Abroad," published in the September 1907 *Putnam's Monthly*, was the first biographical account of his life. William Barrow Floyd mentions West in his book *Jouett, Bush, Frazer: Early Kentucky Artists*. Sara Lewis Flanary wrote a master's thesis on West's career in Natchez and New Orleans, as well as an article for the November 1983 *Antiques* magazine, and we held several conversations on West.

The Frick Art Reference Library, the J. Hall Pleasants Files at the Maryland Historical Society, and the Catalog of American Portraits were the most helpful sources of West's work. The Archives of American Art, Smithsonian Institution, held the only known West letters, either on microfilm or in the Charles Henry Hart Papers. They now have the West papers which I discovered, through the generosity of Mrs. Paul Meissner, West's great-great-grandniece. The J. B. Speed Art Museum, the Corcoran Gallery of Art, and the historical societies of Kentucky, Pennsylvania, Louisiana, Virginia, and New York were very generous with their curatorial and archival materials.

I am very grateful for the many conversations on General Lee that I was able to have with Mary Tyler Freeman Cheek, and the hospitality shown me by Mr. Leslie Cheek, Jr., a wise counsel. Mr. and Mrs. Sewell M. Brumby, Mr. and Mrs. David Burg, Henry and Sally Bruel, Mr. and Mrs. Phineas Stevens, and Jean

Gardiner Chisholm Lindsey so kindly gave me shelter and aid. M. B. Mumford of the Baltimore Museum of Art generously sent me materials on West's Baltimore phase.

Garnett McCoy at the Archives of American Art, and Alan Fern, Ellen Miles, and Robert G. Stewart at the National Portrait Gallery have been my mentors and guides on this project, and I thank them for time, patience, and interest. Mona Dearborn, Diane Blumenthal Winslow, and Jane Yeingst were always supportive at the Catalog of American Portraits. Beverly Jones Cox has been a great help with the exhibition. Frances Stevenson Wein, my editor, proved a kind and tolerant partner. Her efforts on behalf of the catalogue are deeply appreciated. My secretary, Mary Smith, typed my manuscript and held my hand through several rewrites. I am also obliged to the Board of Trustees of the Lauren Rogers Museum of Art for allowing me to pursue this project while serving as their Director.

This volume is dedicated to my grandmother, Carrie Mae Doyle Caywood Logan (1908–1983). She was a woman of deep resources, and I cherish her memory as a bright light of courage and strength. She told wonderful stories, and I developed no small appreciation of the oral tradition from listening to her tales of our family. In a larger sense, this volume is dedicated to the commonwealth of Kentucky, the homeland of the westward-moving pioneers from Virginia, the cradle of horses, tobacco, bourbon whiskey, and Southern sentimentality. William Edward West, in all of his travels, thought of himself as a Kentuckian and reveled in people's strange notions about us.

The work on William Edward West became important to me because I came to feel that he understood the taste of his own time so well. He created a body of portraiture that can be easily separated from other early-nineteenth-century work by a very individual style. His best work has a kind of romantic bravura, by which I mean the fragile human form set forth in heroic terms. I wonder whether any other painter shall so enthrall me.

WILLIAM EDWARD WEST, 1788-1857
KENTUCKY PAINTER

WILLIAM EDWARD WEST, self-portrait, circa 1819. Private collection. [Cat. no. 13]

William Edward West, 1788-1857

William Edward West was born on December 10, 1788, in the frontier town of Lexington, Kentucky, to Edward West, Jr., and his wife, Sarah Creed Brown.[1] Concerning his ancestry, West was always sufficiently vague to encourage the notion that he was related to two fabled figures: Benjamin West, the president of the Royal Academy in England, and William West, rumored to have been the first painter west of the Alleghenies. Actually, he was related to neither. Rather, his ancestors were yeoman farmers and craftsmen in the colonial Southern tradition, who had migrated from England to the Shenandoah Valley of Virginia. William Edward West's grandfather, Edward West, Sr., moved to Scott County, Kentucky, in 1784.

William Edward West's father was a gunsmith, silversmith, and general tinkerer, who followed his family to Kentucky in 1785. By 1788 he had set up shop on High Street, Lexington, as a silversmith, and in 1793 he invented a steamboat which successfully plied the Elkhorn Creek in Fayette County. The creek was small and shallow, however, and the steamboat was not a paddlewheeler, but had instead an inefficient plunging-piston drive shaft unsuitable for navigating more formidable waters. This did not deter his children and grandchildren from substantial resentment of the fame attained shortly thereafter by Robert Fulton. They felt that Edward West should have been acclaimed as Father of the Steamboat. Ironically, William Edward West would later paint Fulton's portrait. Edward West did receive a patent for his steamboat, as well as for a gunlock and a machine for cutting and heading nails.[2]

William Edward West was not born into the kind of log-cabins-to-fame scenario for which Kentucky would become famous in the Jacksonian era. Indeed, Lexington, Kentucky, was celebrated as the "Athens of the West" because of the remarkable assortment of colleges, printing presses, and libraries it possessed. Though not on a major waterway—situated at the crossroads of the old Indian burial and games grounds—Lexington was an important center of commerce and trade, and was the first capital of the state.[3] A contemporary description notes,

"Its streets are laid out at right angles, and are well paved. Few towns are so delightfully situated. Many of the private residences and several of the public edifices are fine specimens of architectural taste."[4] The first college, first library, and first theater west of the Alleghenies were all established there during the first decade of William Edward West's life.

Tobacco, which had made the fortune of colonial Virginia, was being grown in Kentucky, and was shipped down the Kentucky and Ohio rivers to the Mississippi and on to New Orleans. The goods which were received in return for the giant hogsheads, sent down on flatboats, were brought back to Lexington by way of Natchez, Mississippi, and the Natchez Trace trade route. Like many other young men of his time, William Edward West is thought to have been a part of this process. Abram Spears, a wealthy tobacco merchant in adjacent Bourbon County, is credited with taking West and his brother down the Mississippi on one such trek. Whether a miniature of Spears was done by "John B. or William E. West" is uncertain.[5] However, prosperity resulting from this trade made Kentucky a particularly fertile cultural ground, and accounts in part for its rich tradition of antebellum portraiture.

The rise of a visual arts tradition in Kentucky may be credited in part to the appearance of George Beck, landscape painter and portraitist. Beck moved west to Lexington from Cincinnati some time before 1806, when he is listed in the city directory as a portraitist. He and his wife, Mary, taught painting in a girls' seminary, and are thought to have given private instruction to many, including the young West brothers. Beck maintained cultural ties with Philadelphia, where he continued to exhibit until his death in 1812.

Both West boys began as painters of miniatures. Samuel McCullough, a neighbor of the West family in Kentucky, once recounted how "with childish astonishment I saw the bit of ivory under Mr. West's pencil assume on the surface my mother's face so faithfully and truthfully depicted, that I called the miniature my little mama when I was but then five years old."[6] The McCullough miniature is the first work attributed to West, and is said to have been stolen during the War of 1812 from its bearer, a son of the subject.

Of the early portraits painted by West, only two readily identifiable examples remain: those of his father and Dr. Samuel Brown. Brown [Cat. no. 2] was a brother of the United States Senator from Kentucky, John Brown of Liberty Hall in Frankfort. The Brown family had lived in Philadelphia during the first days of the republic, and helped introduce the Federal style to Kentucky through the highly sophisticated architecture of their home, Liberty Hall, the first brick house of substance in the state. Margaret Preston Brown's brother had been painted by Gilbert Stuart, and it is likely that West's first exposure to high-style portraiture occurred in the Brown home.

Dr. Samuel Brown is credited in the family literature, and in the popular literature of the time, as the patron of William Edward West and the source of his means to travel to Philadelphia to "study" with Sully.[7] If Samuel Brown were a near relative of West's, it would not be in the role of uncle or grandfather, as has been suggested. Samuel Brown was born in 1769, making him younger than West's parents. Sarah Brown West, William's mother, was the daughter of another

BATTLE OF NEW ORLEANS, engraving by Yeager after William Edward West, circa 1817. Louisiana State Museum, New Orleans.

Samuel Brown and Maria Creed. It is far more likely that Brown, who attained a certain fame for introducing smallpox vaccine into the plague-ridden Lexington community, was a frequent subject for essaying portraitists, and thus attracted West's attention in what was still a small community.

Dr. Brown left Lexington in 1806 for New Orleans, where he lived until 1809, when he married Miss Catherine Percy of Natchez and moved to that city, remaining there until her death. Brown would have been able to provide excellent contacts in the lower Mississippi valley for the young West, and was from all accounts a very generous man. West must have maintained a close contact with the good doctor, for he instructs his father, in a letter from Florence, Italy, in 1820 (subsequently cited), to greet Dr. Brown. Samuel Brown had returned to Lexington by then to establish a medical college at Transylvania University. West must have painted Brown in 1805–1806, the same period when he painted the likenesses of his father and mother before Brown left Lexington for the deep South and before the artist's journey to Philadelphia and his first encounter with Thomas Sully.

It would not be altogether accurate to say that William Edward West was a pupil of Sully in any formal, academic manner. Sully was only five years older than West, and, at the age of twenty-five in 1808, had no great range of experience or practice for the revered role of teacher. It is more likely that West painted in Sully's studio, observing the artist much as Sully himself had observed Gilbert

Stuart. Thomas Sully's initial association with William Edward West would have been fairly brief, because he left Philadelphia in 1809 for London, where he became a pupil of Benjamin West.

Between his first encounter with Sully, in about 1808, and his departure for Italy in 1819, West began the peripatetic travels for which he would become legendary in his own time. He did keep a studio in Philadelphia from 1809 to 1817, first at Vine and Front Streets, and later, in 1817, moving to 110 North Front Street.

By 1817 West was in New Orleans, a fact substantiated by a record of the painting of the battle of New Orleans, and by a letter written to Thomas Sully, dated January 28, 1817. West introduces the carrier of the letter, a Mr. Evans referred to therein, as "an ardent admirer of painting and one who knows how to value and esteem the talents of the artist."[8] This Mr. Evans was a wealthy Natchez planter known for his patronage of the arts in the lower Mississippi valley. He is also named as a source of the patronage which enabled West to travel to Italy to study. Perhaps the connection was provided by Dr. Samuel Brown, then residing near Natchez.

New Orleans and the entire Delta basin were, at that time, particularly prone to devastating malarial fever sieges. When those fevers occurred, the citizens took refuge on higher ground than the sub-sea-level quarters of the city. During an especially lethal outbreak in 1817, West fled upstream to Natchez, on the bluff above the Mississippi River. William Edward West was to develop a deep attachment to Natchez, and he often referred to it while in Europe.

A newspaper article published in 1881 asserts that in 1800 West was "a boy of but sixteen years of age exhibiting the first evidence of the genius which has since distinguished him as a portrait painter."[9] In that article, West is represented as guest of a Judge Turner, an assertion which seems highly dubious. West was, in fact, twelve years old in 1800, and the Judge Turner mentioned was probably Judge Edward Turner of Natchez, West's subject in later years [Cat. no. 43]

During this early Natchez period, West spent a large amount of time in the company of the prominent Bingaman and Surget families, prefiguring an interesting psychological trend. West developed a pattern of attaching himself to large, prominent families, painting their portraits and injecting himself into their social and cultural life. The Browns of Kentucky were his first attachment, followed by Sully and his family, to whom he makes warm reference in the letter carried by Mr. Evans. "Remember me affectionately to Mr. Sully, wife Sally and the Family. They shall hear from me in due time." West's subsequent relations with the Caton-Patterson families of Baltimore, the Astors of New York, and the Young-Mercer families of Natchez and Louisiana all fall into this pattern. Increasingly, he became a charming, loquacious bachelor pampered by an adoring clan.

West may have needed adoration in 1818, when he apparently contracted some form of the dreaded yellow-fever virus. Writing to his sister, Mrs. Jane Woods of Nashville, he discloses, "I was a good deal sick this summer and spent most of my time at Mrs. Bingamans about four miles from Natchez. She nursed me with the care of a mother."[10] Mrs. Bingaman proved a willing subject, and the result is the finest of West's pre-European career. Ever the teasing wit, West

LETTER, WEST TO THOMAS SULLY, January 28, 1817, New Orleans. Charles Henry Hart Autograph Collection, Archives of American Art, Smithsonian Institution.

continues, *Mrs. Wilkins* [the eldest Bingaman daughter] *has a sister that I used to be pretty much in love with particularly when residing in the same house with her & put up together, as it were. But since I have got well & got my liberty I have got clear of love in the bargain.* The fever had not interfered with his career, as he notes, "I am very much engaged in painting and shall go to Europe in the spring . . . it is probable I may go through Kentucky & start from Philadelphia." Subsequent correspondence with Thomas Sully (from Florence), and a portrait executed in Cincinnati, affirm this route.

EDWARD WEST, JR., by William Edward West, oil on canvas, circa 1805. Nell Foster Waltz. [Cat. no. 1]

The conclusion of West's letter to his sister reveals an interesting character trait: *When I have a good book which would afford me great pleasure in reading, always at my hand—I neglect to do so from the very circumstance of knowing I can do it when I please. It is so in writing to my friends—I neglect it because I know I have it always in my power.*

That throwaway phrase in fact characterized West's early career. Perhaps he had neglected to paint a great deal because he knew that he had it in his power. It would seem that, from late adolescence into his early thirties, West spent a large amount of time wandering about the Old South, showing up here and there, and leaving behind one or two portraits as proof of his residence and ability. Nearly half of his life remains a sketchy outline.

In many respects, the itinerant portraitist played as substantial a pioneering part in the young republic as the migrating yeoman farmer. Both pushed the frontiers of culture ever westward, and both carried with them strong Anglo-American traditions. Portraiture became a valued commodity, and a potent record. In the South, an obsession with family ties created a portrait tradition (or perhaps a tradition of having portraits in the home) that made ancestors into material-culture icons, tender images lovingly passed down from generation to

John Tucker Bowdoin, by William Edward West, oil on canvas, circa 1818. John Page Elliott. [Cat. no. 6]

Thomas R. Fosdick, by William Edward West, oil on panel, 1818. Cincinnati Historical Society, Cincinnati, Ohio, gift of Frank Johnston Jones, 1971. [Cat. no. 12]

generation. William Edward West was no different from many of his contemporaries in having a ready market and an available standard.

Considering style, those works which we know were executed by West before his period with Sully in Philadelphia have a stilted, awkward quality common to many itinerants' work. West had not yet mastered the ability to model the facial contours or to impart to the sitter any subtlety of expression, and created portraits that are little more than a chance encounter between a nervous sitter and a competent, but unsophisticated, artist.

West's portrait of his father, Edward, evinces something of what he may have learned from George and Mary Beck. Though the background and composition lack refinement, the head, for all its flatness, is nicely shaped, and the character, dour and stalwart, is well defined. There is little of the looseness we see in two portraits by West in the late 1810s, however—those of John Tucker Bowdoin and Thomas R. Fosdick.

The portraits of Bowdoin and Fosdick are characterized by long thin noses, large watery eyes, lacy jabots which add light to the picture, and hair tossed rakishly back from the brow. These aspects of style West surely learned from Sully, who himself translated them for his own use from the formula Gilbert Stuart employed with his less notable subjects. Gilbert Stuart employed that formula with great success in his portrait of Mrs. William Robinson, a visage thinly painted, with large dark eyes, a sketchy drapery detail, and a chunky, geometric interpretation of anatomy.

When we compare the portraits of Bowdoin and Fosdick to Thomas Sully's portrait of his brother, Chester, many similarities emerge. The *Fosdick* shares

MRS. WILLIAM ROBINSON, by Gilbert Stuart, oil on panel, 1812. National Gallery of Art, Washington, D.C.

with the Sully portrait a rather pigeon-breasted anatomy, while the Sully and *Bowdoin* portraits have similar facial treatments. All of these were done after Sully had returned from his first trip to England and before West went to Italy. It was also in this period that Sully and West collaborated on a portrait of a Colonel Williams.

The portraits West painted in the lower Mississippi valley fall into two stylistic categories: small formula pictures (dimensions 76.2 x 63.5 cm. [30 x 25 in.]) utilizing a stock pose and coloration, and large (91.9 x 71.1 cm. [36 x 28 in.]), more detailed portraits. The small pictures place the sitters at a distance from the

CHESTER SULLY, by Thomas Sully, oil on panel, 1810. New Orleans Museum of Art, gift of Jeanne Sully West.

picture plane that is great enough to float them high on the canvas. The subject sits within the triangle formed by dividing the picture plane diagonally from its top left to bottom right corners, or vice versa, depending upon whether the sitter is facing left or right. The area above the face is largely negative space, perhaps brushed in by a bit of drapery in the neoclassical manner, or merely a diffuse color field in ochre or brown.

The peculiarity of any portrait is that frozen-in-time aspect wherein the sitter sits eternally fixed, gazing down upon anyone with whatever signature expression has been given him by the artist. Most of the subjects in West's Natchez portraits are gazing out from the corners of their eyes, in a look at once wary and interested. The women—Mrs. Richards and Mrs. Dunbar, for example—both seem slightly amused, while their husbands appear more restrained. In the portraits of Mrs. Richards and Mrs. Bingaman, the same hand, laid palm up with the thumb held in, appears at the bottom of the picture plane, almost like a little dead dove in a still-life painting.

In attitude, the portraits of Mrs. Bingaman and Mrs. Richards bear resem-

SARAH BUCKHOLTZ (MRS. JOHN) RICHARDS, by William Edward
West, oil on canvas, circa 1818. State Historical Museum,
Department of Archives and History, Jackson, Mississippi.
[Cat. no. 11]

MRS. CATHERINE SURGET BINGAMAN, by William Edward West,
oil on canvas, circa 1818. The Art Collection, Tulane
University (Linton-Surget Collection), New Orleans, Louisiana. [Cat. no. 5]

OLIVIA MAGRUDER (MRS. JOSEPH) DUNBAR, by William Edward
West, oil on canvas, circa 1818. Caroline Shields Sessions.
[Cat. no. 9]

FACING PAGE

MARY SICARD DAVID, by Thomas Sully, oil on canvas, 1813.
The Cleveland Museum of Art, gift of the John Huntington
Art and Polytechnic Trust.

blance to a notable Sully of the period, *Mary Sicard David,* in which the hand is held in a similar manner, and the bearing, a combination of a long, elliptical face borne on an equally long neck and oddly shaped shoulder raised quite high above the collarbone, became a standard convention.

In many respects, the portrait of Mrs. Bingaman is the most finished in this period, perhaps accounted for by the artist's long stay in her Natchez home. It is the only known West work in this first period with an atmospheric landscape, complete with a rocaille tree and a distant, misty horizon appearing behind the drapery. Though West had described Mrs. Bingaman in motherly terms in the letter to his sister, she was only twelve years his senior. She looks a little shrewd and a little wise, no young coquette in high-society Natchez, yet lively and dimpled under her lace cap and curls.

In his wanderings from Lexington to Philadelphia and back down to New Orleans and Natchez, West employed a portrait style derived from the masters of the period. He demonstrated a talent personalized by his own virtuoso abilities with paint, as latent and indolently employed as his letter writing—"close at hand and seldom practised."

Late in 1819, William Edward West sailed for Europe to undertake formal training in painting at the Academy in Florence. Although the exact date of his departure is uncertain, two extant letters reveal something of his route. Writing from Florence to his father in February of 1820, he remarks that he "had a pleasant voyage of only twenty-six days in coming, as I wrote you from Havre, France." [11]

By what means William Edward West traveled to Europe, to begin his studies at the age of thirty-one, has been the subject of much speculation.[12] In some accounts Dr. Samuel Brown is his sponsor, and indeed the postscript to the letter to his father adds, "Give my respects to Dr. Brown." Other accounts have him traveling to Italy with the previously mentioned Mr. Evans of Natchez, connoisseur and collector.

However he found himself in Europe, this rambling raconteur from the frontier saw little to excite him or to mark him out as unsophisticated. *I arrived here* [Florence] *. . . after travelling through France, Switzerland, Savoy & & & without seeing anything very wonderful,* he wrote in the letter to his father, *and I have not been here long enough to give you an account of any of the wonders of this place. I have seen different gallerys of paintings but so superficially that I will not pretend to say anything about them. I must tell you tho I have seen Sir Thos. Lawrence and a number of his best paintings—many of the Kings and other bloods of Europe.*

West had arrived in Europe at a critical juncture. In 1820 George III died, as did Benjamin West. This marked not only the ascent to the throne of the gaudy regent, George IV (whose court painter Sir Thomas Lawrence proved to be), but also Lawrence's own rise to the Presidency of the Royal Academy. Lawrence's influence certainly seems apparent in the romantic, windblown treatment of hair and the lush coloration of Thomas Sully, traits which were transmitted to the impressionable West. While William Edward West was in Europe, Lawrence became the greatest force in the Anglo-American portraiture tradition.

Ironically, Sir Thomas Lawrence and West were in Italy at the same time. Lawrence was completing his series of portraits of the allies who defeated Napoleon. Those Grand-Manner portraits would later be installed in the Waterloo Chamber at Windsor Castle. Having set up his studio at Aix-la-Chapelle, he painted, among other notables, the Emperors of Austria and Russia; thus West's viewing of "Kings and other bloods." In late 1819 and early 1820, he was being lionized in Rome, where he painted Pope Pius VII. Apparently he was made a fellow of the Academy at Florence, for when he returned to England, in March of 1820, he began to add to his list of honors "Member of the Academy of Fine Arts, Florence." He was elected President of the Royal Academy immediately upon his return.

West's choice of the Academy at Florence as a place of study reveals considerable perception and motivation in an artist already in full maturity. The oldest art academy in existence, the Academy at Florence offered several advantages to the developing artist, for the instruction was theoretical, teaching techniques of revered artists while offering painting and drawing in life classes. There was the added advantage of being able to observe and copy Old Master paintings, notably Titian and the mannerist painters in the galleries of the Uffizi, the Pitti Palace, and other Florentine collections.

With a bravura noblesse oblige, West comments to his father, *There is no painter in Italy equal to Lawrence, if that is what we are after. But here are the old masters and here is nature in perfection. As for the Academy it might be better. There are no lectures on anatomy, yet for a man with a light pocket Florence has much to recommend it. One can live here for very little and the finest models always before him at the same price.* The comment on lectures indicates that no formal programs on human anatomy were held, yet there seems to have been an obvious emphasis on rendering from life. That analysis may be backed up by West's professed procurement of the finest models. "There is an immense number of the finest paintings in the world," he writes his father.

An amusing disparity arises between West's communication to his old friend and partner, Sully, and to his father. West writes to Sully of the ease of acquiring "A pair of elegant furnished rooms . . . for $4 a month."[13] To his father he boasts, *In a pleasant quiet part of town I have rented the wings of one of the most beautiful palaces in Florence, consisting of twenty or thirty apartments, not finished. It contains several superb rooms, with north lights, exactly adapted for painting in. For this reason, I hired it and could not hire a part of it but was obliged to take the whole, and a good painting room was to be had nowhere else. You may think me extravagant, but I assure you I give no more than $6 a month for the whole wing, to take it by the year, as I have done.*

West lived at number 12 Via Sancti Apostoli in the rooms he described to Sully, in a *palazzo* that would house his fellow-Kentuckian, the sculptor Joel Tanner Hart.[14] Edward West, whose other children were safely married, prosperous, bourgeois merchants, may have found the vagaries of an itinerant artist son disconcerting. West seems anxious to demonstrate his own prosperity, sending back the kind of embellished tall tales reminiscent of the frontier humor of the Old South.

WILLIAM EDWARD WEST'S RESIDENCE IN FLORENCE, number 12 Via Sancti Apostoli, reproduced in Clara Louise Dentler, *Famous Foreigners in Florence 1400–1900* (1964).

Nonetheless, William Edward West seems to have been seriously studying his craft. He tells his father, "I employ my time at present in drawing from the statues and learning Italian, but shall not paint much until I get into my new Quarters." He was not unconscious of the scenery or of the art he had at hand. *The town is situated in the most beautiful valley in the world. Surrounded by mountains covered with olive trees and vineyards, among which are scattered hundreds of the most beautiful palaces. It is built on both sides of the River Arno and above and below it the borders are lined by gardens and fruit trees and nothing can exceed the prospect in beauty or the climate in healthfulness.*

Americans abroad were considered a great curiosity, and West wrote to his father, "An American coming this far to study the fine arts is considered by the inhabitants a great compliment paid to their city, and of course I meet with every civility I could wish." West's feelings for them differed substantially: "I am sorry I cannot say as much in favor of the inhabitants as of their country. They are a degenerate race." He leaves little doubt that the days of Florentine greatness were past, and Florence had become the first modern tourist spot. He writes that "2000 rich English families pass through and reside in Florence every year."

Perhaps the most puzzling aspect of West's letter to Sully is the request that he makes for supplies. He seems to have found, in the city of great painters and great museums, no artist's equipment to his liking. At great length he describes to Sully the kind of paint box "of the finest mahogany" he should like—"as complete as possible, put everything in it even to a pair of pinchers and awl." He further requests "eight pallet knives, 3 for grinding paint of the larger size and 5 of different small sizes for the pallet." Showing the same disdain for Italian craftsmen as he does for their domestic cousins, West notes, "it would make you laugh to see the implements they use here for paintings."

It was while he was in Florence that William Edward West was asked to

GEORGE NOEL GORDON, LORD BYRON, by William Edward West, oil on canvas, 1822. National Portrait Gallery, Edinburgh, Scotland. [Cat. no. 14]

paint a portrait of George Noel Gordon, Lord Byron. This would prove to be the most important commission in the artist's life. According to West's own account, he was approached by Mr. George K. Bruen to paint a portrait of Byron for the American Academy in New York.[15] Mr. Bruen must have been an acquaintance of West's in Florence, for in a letter to Byron he asks permission for "my friend Mr. West of Mississippi" to paint the portrait. It could be that West had met Mr. Bruen through his friend Mr. Evans, from Natchez, and thus the Mississippi connection. "I would not have ventured to intrude this request upon your Lordship's patience—if I did not know how much we should value in our own country a portrait of Lord Byron painted by an American, who has already obtained at home some reputation in his art." [16]

Some reputation would be correct, but how much is questionable. The selection of West to paint, for an American audience, a portrait of the greatest living poet is a happenstance not unlike overnight success. Though West may have had some visibility in Philadelphia through his connection with Sully, he had exhibited at the Pennsylvania Academy only once, in 1817—a portrait of St. Peter, now lost, which may have been a copy of a Raphael. He certainly enjoyed "some reputation" among the planter class of the lower South, but that would hardly have afforded him acclaim; merely bed, board, and a modest income.

It is far more likely that the ever-social and chatty West, prone to wandering and socializing, had made the acquaintance of Mr. Bruen in Florence, showing him drawings while spinning tall tales of the sort that he wrote to his father, and would later tell Lord Byron.

In 1822, when the portrait was commissioned, Lord Byron was dallying in Italy in the company of his mistress, Teresa, Countess Guiccioli, of the noble Gamba family of Ravenna. Byron had been absent from England for some six years, leaving amid the scandal surrounding the collapse of his marriage in 1816. He would never see England again. He met Teresa Guiccioli in Venice in 1819, where she was visiting with her husband, a wealthy Count forty years her elder.

Byron was very popular with the American public. Though not as popular as Sir Walter Scott, he commanded a substantial audience, and in 1822 his works were selling enough throughout the English-speaking world to guarantee his freedom from England. There his reputation was under a cloud stemming from the accusation of incest with his half-sister.

Byron had been at Leghorn, the Italian resort where West would paint him, beginning early in 1822, in the company of the adventurer-poet Edward John Trelawny, and the Shelley, Hunt, and Gamba families. Countess Guiccioli's family had been exiled by the Pope from their own estate for republican activities and the Carbonari conspiracy.[17] Leigh Hunt, his wife, and his children were being supported by Byron, and they had hopes of establishing a literary review. Shelley was living quietly by the sea, and would be dead from drowning by midsummer. William Edward West happened upon the final act of the romantic movement.

As with Byron's life, the sitting, and the episodes attendant upon it, were full of exciting melodrama. In an account of the portrait sitting, published in London in the *New Monthly Magazine* in 1826, William Edward West describes the sitting in great detail.[18] His expectation of the encounter is invested with an air of romantic grandeur. "I expected to see a person somewhat thin and swarthy with a high forehead and black curly hair with the countenance severe and stern and manners reserved and lofty." As is so often the case, West was severely disappointed. "I was mistaken and much surprised to see almost the reverse of what I had imagined."

Lord Byron was living at the Villa Rossa in Monte Nero, four miles from Leghorn. He had recently had a triumphant visit to the U.S.S. *Constitution,* moored offshore. That visit became the subject for West's only known nautical painting, perhaps rendered at a later date in order to capitalize upon the notoriety of his connection with Byron. Byron shared the Villa Rossa with the Hunt and Gamba families, including Countess Guiccioli's brother, who would accompany him on his journey to Greece. West notes that the house was so full that Byron "expressed much regret that he could not have me at his house altogether there being a family of friends with him at the time and his house being very small." The initial interview was finished off by a pleasant lunch, and West left, "much pleased with our visit."

The following day, they began the portrait, West finding Byron "a bad sitter . . . he talked almost all the time . . . when he didn't talk he was a worse sitter for he assumed a countenance that did not belong to him." West was pleased with the proceedings, however, feeling "nothing like fear or embarrassment in the company of this great man—he was so perfectly simple in his manners—so free and easy and even familiar and friendly that I parted with him quite delighted." West's reports of Byron's eating habits are in accord with various biographical notes on the poet, who suffered a tendency to fatness. He ate sparely, "only a little bread dipped in mustard— and drank little or nothing."

While Byron was sitting to West, Countess Guiccioli appeared, impressing the painter with her beauty. "I thought I had never seen a more romantic looking head." Byron soon asked West to paint the Countess as well, and in subsequent sessions they posed alternately, Byron being pleased with both likenesses. "Throughout the sitting Byron was restless, speaking at once of his frustrations with England, what England would not do for him and what he would not do for England. He also lapsed into attacks of melancholy as unfavorable reviews of his work appeared in the mails."

William Edward West found Byron to have an immense interest in America and things American. He was very familiar with the writings of Washington Irving, who had been well received in England, and frequently quoted the sayings of Knickerbocker, Irving's hero. Byron thought that "an American ought to have a straight forward simplicity of manners, incorruptibility, deference for customs and governments of other countries, but no affection for them." Byron tried to trick West into uttering American colloquial expressions, but, as West slyly remarks, could never make him say "I guess."

It has been suggested that West may have told Byron stories of the frontier hero, Daniel Boone, during the course of the sitting, and this would account for the presence of the Kentuckian in *Don Juan*.[19] West does mention that Byron was working on the epic *Don Juan* throughout the sittings, showing him the "sixth and seventh (I think) Cantos of Don Juan in manuscript." If West did indeed speak of old Kentucky, he makes no mention of it in his account; but then the account concentrates on West's impression of Byron, and not on the details of his own conversation.

Furthermore, the account itself was written after Byron's death, and was published in 1826, by which time West may have found the time or occasion to embellish the account considerably. West's handwritten version of the portrait sitting adventure differs slightly from the printed version in the *New Monthly Magazine*, but there is still no mention of conversations concerning Kentucky or Daniel Boone.

West told Byron that he did not find him a happy man. The poet *inquired earnestly what reason I had for thinking so and I asked him if he had never observed in little children after a paroxysm of grief, that they had at intervals a convulsive or tremulous manner of drawing in a long breath. Wherever I had observed this in persons of whatever age, I had always found that it came from sorrow.*

Considering Byron's chaotic life, such sighs do not seem especially extraordinary. Exiled from his homeland by choice, encamped by the sea with a huge party of whom he was the sole support, and entangled with a married woman whose husband was now threatening murder, Byron was surely besieged. His predicament was further complicated by an episode which occurred during the portrait-painting process.

An irate Italian, perhaps vexed at republican leanings in the Byron-Gamba household, had wounded one of Byron's servants in a brawl. Count Gamba rushed out to his defense. *In a few moments we heard the screaming of a female, and on hastening into the hall, beheld Count Gamba with a pistol in each hand and covered with blood. The Guiccioli was greatly agitated, and rushed to prevent her brother from going into the yard; then seized hold of Lord Byron and then turned to me and entreated me not to desert them, for that they were all going to be murdered.*

All of this West found most predictable, murder being a "very natural supposition, for their lives had often been threatened in anonymous letters and the present disturbance did not seem unlike a conspiracy to carry those threats into effect." The incident brought to a close the association with Byron, for, "according to the usual practice of Italian justice, which appears to find that the best mode of settling disputes is to punish both parties," the Gamba family was asked to leave Tuscany. Lord Byron packed up with his entourage and departed. He and West would never meet again.

The Byron and Guiccioli portraits remained in the hands of William Edward West, ostensibly for finishing touches, but becoming a source of capital. Taking leave of Lord Byron, William Edward West had "an impression that he possessed an excellent heart, which had been misconstrued on all hands from little else than a reckless levity of manners, which he took a whimsical pride in opposing to those of others."

Characterization aside, the painterly technique of the portraits of Byron and his mistress reveal the impact of West's Florentine training. When he left frontier Mississippi for Europe, his painting style evidenced a certain understanding of the prevailing high style of Stuart and Sully. To that manner may be added the forms derived from his admiration of Lawrence. The Byron portrait is a transition picture. The figure is still placed very high on the picture plane; the barely visible hand in the original of many copies is static, and only barely protrudes from the swirls and folds of the cloak enveloping the lyric poet.

West found Byron's head "apparently effeminate, his complexion delicate, his eyes light blue or grey, and his hair dark brown combed smoothly over his forehead and falling with a few curls down about his neck." So West painted him. The facial modeling is smoother and more fully contoured, while the mood of

Flora, by Titian, circa 1515. Uffizi, Florence, Italy.

Teresa Gamba, Countess Guiccioli, by William Edward West, oil on canvas, 1822. Miami University Art Museum, Miami, Ohio, gift of Jonathan S. Bishop. [Cat. no. 15]

the picture is substantially more sophisticated than West's earlier work. The portrait has a grand quality, enhanced by the bravura of the opened, white-collared shirt from which Byron's neck protrudes swanlike to a delicately featured face. West captured something of Byron's androgynous nature, for the lips are thinly drawn, stopping short of a pout, and the nose is thin, aquiline, aristocratic.

The portrait of the Countess Guiccioli is a far more radical departure from the frontier style, more Italianate in manner, and especially evocative of Titian in composition, coloration, and pose. Titian's *Flora*, an extremely popular paint-ing which West would have seen repeatedly in the Uffizi, seems one source for the Guiccioli portrait. Both women have their hair parted in the center, falling back off their faces, and reddish curls spilling over their shoulders. West has painted Teresa Guiccioli's face as an elliptical configuration inclined to the left, eyes gazing upward in the same direction. It is nearly the same pose as the *Flora*, though in reverse—even to the similarity of the hand protruding from the sleeve of the garment as a highly stylized afterthought. As in the *Flora*, the *Guiccioli* is painted in historical garb—a high-Renaissance gown, complete with puffed sleeves, slit to allow the showing of a lighter cloth lining, along with the inevitable floating drapery wandering around the right shoulder and absently parallelling the hand.

Following the *Byron*, West's portraits begin to take on a depth of characterization that had previously been missing. His infatuation with intricate mannerist composition would have begun in Florence, the birthplace of mannerism. West's subsequent genre and literary paintings are often very ambitious compositions, highly mannered and not always successful.

His postponed student days behind, West left Florence in 1824 to open a studio in Paris. There he would have a certain vogue as the last painter to depict Byron from life. Byron's ill-fated journey to Greece in 1823 had ended with his death in fever-ridden Missoulonghi, leaving West free to regale several salons with the details, real and otherwise, of their encounter. He was but one of the two notable American raconteurs in Paris, however, competing with Betsy Patterson Bonaparte.

As an American abroad, and with newfound fame, William Edward West would certainly have made his way into the salon of Elizabeth Patterson Bonaparte.[20] She was the daughter of a prominent Baltimore merchant, and the erstwhile wife of Jerome Bonaparte. The Emperor Napoleon had not approved the marriage between his brother and this American in 1803. After producing a son, Jerome Napoleon Bonaparte, while exiled in England, she went home to America, never to see her husband again. With the fall of the Napoleonic regime in 1815, Betsy Bonaparte returned to France and took up residence there until 1840. She was a celebrated wit, whose salon was frequented by both French and American luminaries.

Elizabeth Patterson's brother Edward, the representative of the family trade in France in 1825, was visiting his sister there, accompanied by the widow of his elder brother, Elizabeth Caton Patterson, later Marchioness of Wellesley. Mrs. Patterson was from yet another wealthy Baltimore merchant family, and was one of three Caton sisters, celebrated for their beauty as the "Three Graces." Many of West's future commissions, indeed those which provided the most stable income that he would have over the next twenty years, came from the vast network of Caton-Patterson family connections.

In Paris, Washington Irving again enters West's life. Irving's journals (during the years 1824 and 1825) provide some details on the emerging Baltimore alliance between West and the Caton-Patterson clan. These were rather backwater years for him, between the success of *The Sketch Book* and the critical acclaim in England, and his appointment to the diplomatic post in Spain. Irving had been a great admirer of Lord Byron, grieving at his death and mourning at his passing into the "heaven of narration." [21]

Irving's journals frequently mention visits to West's studio. *December 25, 1824 — Called at Mr. West's — Mrs. Patterson sitting for her picture — Lynch there—stayed until half past three. February 5th, 1825—Mr. Lynch and Miss Caton sitting. February 10th—Called at West's, found the daughter-in-law and granddaughters of LaFayette there — accompanied the Storrows to see West's pictures. February 16th. Called on West—had much conversation about Lord Byron.*[22]

West was gaining a reputation as a painter of American travelers abroad, a reputation enhanced by the Byron portrait. This he kept in his studio for sitters to remark upon. It is also likely at this time that West began a painting which has come to be called *The Muses of Painting, Poetry, and Music,* a beautifully colored allegory in a very mannered style.

In *The Muses,* the lessons of the years in Florence come through most brilliantly as West essays the conventions he has learned. A vase of flowers on the table would be repeated frequently in portraits executed in the Baltimore and New York periods, after his return to America. The putti pulling the cord of the drapery on the right is baroque in manner, as is the cherub peering in through the window on the left, which opens onto an atmospheric landscape with a temple high on the hill, in the Italian tradition. The figure symbolizing Music holds a guitar, while the figure symbolizing Painting holds a brush. Both objects rush out from the picture plane towards the viewer, creating a depth of perspective and visual arrangement which borders on the disturbing. The faces of the figures, while locked into the classic triangular construction, are slightly unrelated. The two figures stacked on the left, Painting and Poetry, seem to be gazing, slightly in awe, at the figure of Music.

If these figures are indeed intended to be the three Caton sisters, as the surviving family literature indicates, West is surely suggesting the awe in which the younger sisters held the eldest. She is peering straight out of the canvas, her head cast to one side, and one hand is gracefully extended, about to strum the strings of the guitar. The hand has an extreme, tapering length. The chair upon which she sits has a brightly finished surface, and the fabric is painted in great detail. An intricate, well-wrought composition, the painting is made more amusing by a certain pretentious use of material culture.

A mandolin, perhaps, but not a guitar, would seem more appropriate for a high-style allegory. True, guitars do appear in the hands of young women in Southern itinerant portraits, but not in the hands of a young woman wearing a jewelled tiara upon her head. Odd, too, is the holding of the paintbrush by the figure on the left. It is held in a manner—extending out from the body, grasped between the thumb and forefinger—which would make it entirely useless for painting. The poetic figure in the rear, half in light and half in shadow, is grasping a minute quill which looks *just plucked* from a passing pigeon.

The Muses has a tremendous vitality of the type which arises when an American, and a frontier American at that, attempts to appropriate a European, academic, high style and translate it into a viable art form. The intention of the painting is unclear. If it was indeed intended as a portrait of the young Caton sisters, it partakes slightly of certain late-eighteenth-century English neoclassical portrait conventions, quoted in an Italianate fashion. The redoubtable putti, one of whom rises, rather full-figured, to pull the drape, and one of whom is staring on in somewhat indolent adoration, are Baroque motifs. West seems, here, to be determined to embark upon a career as a sophisticated painter and portraitist, borne aloft by his Byron connection, and strengthened by the number of commissions executed in Paris in an ambitious style.

The lure of London, and of a likely celebrity as "Byron's last portraitist," induced West to leave Paris. He departed on May 9, 1825, preceded by the Caton-Patterson clan.[23]

London, in the reign of George IV, seems to have been to West's liking, for Irving's letter responds to a remark that West must have made about the "natural-ness" of London as opposed to Paris. "I am glad you are much pleased with London, particularly its sidewalks and chambermaids . . . I will not contend with the point as to which of the two cities is more natural as to scenery or inhabitants."[24]

West entered London society enthusiastically. He seems to have made the most of his portrait of Byron, commenting that "This is the picture which has made me famous" in a letter to Peter Irving.[25] He met many of the English and American painters then living in London as a result of it. Washington Irving had given him a letter of introduction to the Anglo-American painter Charles Robert Leslie, then becoming well known for his portraits and English history pictures.[26] The history and genre painting of Leslie and of David Wilkie were to have a great impact on West.[27] He attempted several genre paintings while in England, as well as paintings derived from Washington Irving's stories.

Three distinct episodes were to mark the London period of William Edward West: he met the poetess Felicia Hemans, with whom he developed a strong relationship; he entered into business dealings with the Caton sisters, which led to his bankruptcy; and he began to show his work at the Royal Academy, and pursued a painting style which led to his final maturation as a painter.

Felicia Hemans was introduced to West by an entrepreneur who was

THE MUSES OF PAINTING, POETRY, AND MUSIC, by William Edward West, oil on canvas, circa 1825. The Corcoran Gallery of Art, Washington, D.C., gift of Elizabeth H. E. McNabb in memory of Sarah West Norvell Leonard. [Cat. no. 19]

establishing a portrait gallery of notable Englishmen of the day.[28] Mrs. Hemans was a poetess of some note, whose husband had deserted her early on, leaving her with five small sons and no income. She resorted to living with several of her relatives, producing volumes of Romantic poetry very much in the Byron-Shelley mode, and attracting a large following in England and America. Whether really ill or merely self-deceived, Mrs. Hemans became a semi-invalid, and by the time West met her she was more or less bedridden.

Sitting to West for a portrait seems to have had a strong impact upon Mrs. Hemans, who developed a great attachment to him. In several letters she pours out her heart to him in a most plaintive manner, frank enough to cause great suspicion in descendant generations of West's family. With a kind of Victorian

FELICIA HEMANS, by William Edward West. Unlocated. Reproduced in
Putnam's Monthly, September 1907. Archives of American Art,
Smithsonian Institution.

prudishness, they closely guarded the letters that she had written to him, obscuring, for fear of scandal, the biographical importance of the exchange.

Felicia Hemans had a great flair for the dramatic and the desperate: *There is always an ideal of beauty, and passion, and music, within me, which I can never embody in language, it is as if a sweet song went floating past me, the expression of which I could not catch or repeat. If I were happier, perhaps I could attain far higher excellence, but no power of mind can prevent woman from being a dependent creature, and that want of a voice and an eye to cheer me on is the thought of sorrow into which all my efforts die away. I must not dream of happiness.. I can only hope for alleviation.*[29]

The departure of Captain Hemans for a tour of Italy in 1818, from which he did not return, was sufficient cause for her unhappiness. He had been a poor provider from the beginning. Throughout their marriage, the budding Hemans brood had continued to live at Bronwylfa, the home of her eldest brother, due to impecunity. Captain Hemans was a veteran of the Napoleonic wars, and it was suggested that his health and stamina had been weakened by that experience. Discreet Victorian observance could not fathom why he did not respond to so pleasant a residence as Bronwylfa, "with a wife, five sons, and a resident mother-in-law." [30] The Hemanses had been married in 1812, and by 1818 Captain Hemans saw fit to remove to Italy, from whence he never returned, nor saw his wife or children again. The poetess's sister, Mrs. Hughes, writing in a biography of her sister, thought that perhaps the "marital deportment of the Captain" led to the separation. "It is, however, unfortunately but too well known that such were not the only reasons which led to the divided course." [31]

When Felicia Hemans sat for her portrait to West in 1827, her husband had been gone for nine years. Her affection for West became highly developed after the sittings, when an interest in the likeness for publication in several souvenir volumes led to some consternation on the artist's part. She writes, "I am very glad that you refused the picture in my name for the souvenir; remember, my friend, that in any point connected with it I have no wish but yours." [32]

The personal depth of that wish is even more apparent when she sends him some lines on the painting, remarking, "They may be shown to anyone you like, but there are allusions in them which only you can fully understand." [33] We may wonder how fully he responded to her entreaties. *My friend, who I have trusted beyond all others, you know the power of suffering there is within me, leave me not in this suspense, my mind and health are sinking under it, I have not been able to leave my room these three days—only free me from this anxiety—and tell me that I still possess your esteem and I will strive to be myself again.* [34] West's attentions were so vital to her that "it is only in your kindness I can find relief from the vain regrets which I have allowed so to prey upon my mind." These, we assume, would be the regrets attendant upon her failed marriage and her dependency upon her family for support.

In 1829, after the death of her mother, Felicia Hemans lived for a while near Liverpool. She visited Scotland, making the acquaintance of Sir Walter Scott, and finally went to reside with her younger brother in Dublin in 1831. She was befriended by Archbishop Whatley, and there are many references to West sending letters to her in care of the "Palace," in order that her family might not know of their correspondence. When proper—as when her brother knew that West would be writing to respond to a question concerning the use of the portrait, one version of which he had kept in his possession—West was instructed to write to her directly. The tone of the letters suggests a secret correspondence between the increasingly ailing poetess and the celebrated artist.

Just how much of this air of secrecy and high romance was a product of a lonely woman, a measure of the manners of the time, or the genuine interest of William Edward West, we really have no way of knowing. Later generations of West's family believed that Mrs. Hemans had been his great love. They wanted to shield him from any scandal following a romance with a woman who, though deserted, remained married. Charles Henry Hart, the art historian, referred to the portrait of Mrs. Hemans as being of someone "with whom he is believed to have had a grande passion." [35] But these speculations are merely a part of the oral tradition surrounding West. From West himself, we have nothing, save the fact that of the three portraits he made of Felicia Hemans, he kept one of them for the rest of his life.

If he did care for her deeply, either the demands and constraints of her family, or his wandering nature, of which we have already witnessed forty years on two sides of the Atlantic, kept them apart. Frequent references, in her letters, to

THE PRESENT, by William Edward West, oil on canvas, 1833. The J. B. Speed Art Museum, Louisville, Kentucky. [Cat. no. 25]

his presence at various country houses involved with this or that person indicate that he was indeed quite occupied and increasingly peripatetic. Mrs. Hemans teasingly suggests that she "must certainly begin to imagine that you are gone to paint the Emperor of China and his wives, or at least to dine with some of your friends on the banks of the Mississippi." [36] It cannot be imagined that her constant clutching comments, imploring him to write or visit, would have helped the situation a great deal.

In the same letter, Felicia Hemans cautions West to "finish those pictures as soon as you can," as "some person or other is trying to spread a deprecating tone about you in the country." The letters in West's portfolio indicate that he was

ANNETTE DELARBRE, by William Edward West, oil on canvas, 1831. Munson-Williams-Proctor Institute, Utica, New York. [Cat. no. 24]

indeed accepting a great many invitations. From what we already know of his character, it is not unlikely that he was spending far more time being social than he was actually painting, or, for that matter, finishing his portrait commissions. He was regularly exhibiting genre and literary pictures as well as portraits throughout this period, at the Royal Academy and the British Institution.

Of the non-portrait work, *The Present* and *Annette Delarbre* are the most notable, for both depart from a mannerist interest in perspective. Following his English contemporaries, he affirms the flat, two-dimensionality of the picture plane. *The Present* and *Annette Delarbre* are almost friezes, each occupied by a horizontal band of figures, across the middle third of the picture plane, expressing a large variety of attitudes. Both have strong central themes.

In *The Present*, a young girl examines a gift of a beautiful necklace. Framing the lovely central figure, her head cast down demurely to admire the necklace, are two matronly figures, presumably the mother on the left, wearing a cap and looking up expectantly at the reaction of the beneficiary. Another matronly figure on the left appears to be a servant, also in a cap, wearing a shawl, and escorting, at her right side, a young boy who is looking out of the picture. On the young girl's right, three other maidens have facial expressions varying from obvious envy to coy wonder, while a partially hidden figure on the left attempts to peer over the subject's shoulder at the necklace, a strand of amethysts set in scalloped gold. A rather wild-eyed dog in the lower right is locked into a visual interaction with the figures of the boy and the servant woman, and heightens the comic aspect. The painting is one of West's best works, a virtuoso statement of his ability to convey various modes of expression while balancing these characters in a rather crowded setting.

The literary painting *Annette Delarbre*, drawn from the Washington Irving short story, is also an expanded frieze of faces. *Annette* was exhibited at the Royal Academy in 1832, and brought West acclaim equal to the notoriety he had achieved for the Byron portrait. It was always the picture that he is thought to have liked best, and the one which he felt made his reputation in England. It is surely the most finished of West's paintings, from the modeling of the fabric folds in the gowns of the women and the frock coat of the old gentleman, to the atmospheric landscape background, executed in the moody manner of John Constable. The central figure of the painting is again, as in *The Present*, a young woman, but in this case a young woman numbed by grief and apparently dazed. She is surrounded by a number of her fellow-villagers and relations, all of them peering in upon her, which has the effect of drawing us as the viewers into the center of the picture, across many faces, as though we, too, were a part of the scene.

Annette Delarbre attracted the attention of the poet Samuel Rogers, and led to West's introduction into various other levels of English culture and society. He was invited to the homes of many in the financial community, including the Baring family of the investment house. With his ongoing friendships in the American community and the remnants of the Byron circle, he had ample opportunity for storytelling. The Caton sisters were firmly settled in England, and his involvement with them continued to be a dominant thread in his life.

By 1830 the names of Aaron Vail, Thomas Aspinwall, and Joshua Bates begin to appear more frequently in West's portfolio. He seems to have enjoyed access to the American diplomatic and financial community in London, which was then struggling to assert its national interests. Andrew Jackson's machinations at that time with a national bank of America had done very little to help the international standing of United States currency; and a good deal of American venture capital was coming from the city of London. Many American firms were either sending representatives or family members abroad to manage their interests.

The larger group with whom West came into contact included the Baltimore merchant families he met through his Patterson-Caton connections. This network was strengthened by the appointment of Louis McLane to the ministership in 1829, for he had extensive interests in the Delaware Valley and in Baltimore city. It is important to note that in 1830 the greatest American export was Southern cotton for the mills of England.[37] West, with his deep-South background, was surely at home among those protecting and developing Southern interests. As

WILLIAM EDWARD WEST, self-portrait, oil on canvas, circa 1835. Unlocated. Reproduced in *Putnam's Monthly*, September 1907. Archives of American Art, Smithsonian Institution.

his community became more financial and less artistic, West began to search for an investment scheme of his own.

During his last five years in England, William Edward West participated in speculations concerning a pneumatic railway device invented by a fellow American, Jacob Perkins. Perhaps drawn to Perkins by American kinship and by memories of his father's endeavors, West became deeply involved in a bubble. This buildup of large amounts of venture capital, in a project which ultimately failed, ruined West's fortunes and caused his return to America.

Jacob Perkins, the inventor mentioned in several letters on the speculation, exchanged between the Caton sisters and West, had begun as a banknote engraver. He had arrived in England in 1819, when he—along with Charles Heath, the English engraver, and Gideon Fairman, his American printing partner—founded a firm specializing in banknote printing. In 1823 Perkins began to experiment with high-pressure steam engines and boilers that used tubes of circulating water to achieve pressure as high as two thousand pounds. This would have produced the intense energy required to power a steam locomotive or "pneumatic railroad." Apparently, he began to seek support for an English patent, as well as for several international patents. He also sought financial support in the American community, for which he used William Edward West as a willing agent.

Letters to West, in this period, from the Caton sisters contain many references to Perkins, as do those from other correspondents, including William Noskins of the American legation. Mary Caton Patterson Wellesley was particularly interested, for "No one will feel more proud that an American should have the glory of the invention, or that you should be enabled to enjoy all that wealth can give." [38]

West's need to improve his financial standing is understandable. In 1832 he had been in Europe for thirteen years, knocking about as much as he had on the

Mississippi twenty years earlier. His efforts to capitalize upon the Byron portrait had been only partially successful. Dunlap, in his account of West, felt that he *experienced some disappointment in respect to selling this portrait of Byron, which he brought to London thinking no price too high for John Bull to give for the acknowledgedly best likeness of the popular poet. He refused a very liberal offer, (I am afraid to say how much) and the public feeling fell and the value of Byron's head with it.*[39]

West finally sold the original of the Byron portrait to Lord Malmesbury in 1829, in an effort to raise money, and for a price less than the two thousand dollars he had required earlier. As to fees, one sitter remarked that she "knows the price for my portrait is fifty guineas."[40] In the English money of the 1830s, that would be an adequate sum, but not one conducive to a lifestyle spent amongst the wealthy and aristocratic. Furthermore, previous evidence from Felicia Hemans indicates that West was not producing a large body of work; nor was he creating a good image of himself as a prompt and efficient portraitist. He seems to have enjoyed lolling about country houses and conversing with the grand at the expense of his art. While he was a regular exhibitor at the Royal Academy from 1826 to 1832, his portrait of Aaron Vail in 1833 is the last of his work to appear there (Vail was then chargé d'affaires of the American legation in London).

West's increased interest in the financial and diplomatic arenas may account for his services to Aaron Vail as a diplomatic courier. He was given a diplomatic visa to carry dispatches abroad on three different occasions. In December of 1832 he carried dispatches to France, and again to that country in 1834; in April of 1833 he was carrying dispatches to the Hague. All of this activity may have been in connection with explorations for a patent for Perkins's steam engine. Mary Wellesley had mentioned the Holland patent with the cogent remark "What will it do in Holland where there already are Canals?"[41]

The intensity of the Caton sisters' involvement with West in these ventures may be accounted for by the fact that they, too, were living among the wealthy aristocrats of England on limited means. Mary Caton Patterson had married the Duke of Wellington's brother, Richard, in 1825, becoming, in the words of her sister Elizabeth, "one of the loveliest Vice-Queens the Irish ever had."[42] The Marquess had been the Lord Lieutenant of Ireland since 1822. Washington Irving commented upon that matter with interest, as he hoped that West's association with the Caton sisters would "get him into a run of fashionable and lucrative patronage."[43]

The finances of the Catons were fixed by the will of their grandfather, the fabulously wealthy Charles Carroll of Carrollton, America's first millionaire. Elizabeth Caton bemoaned the fact that "I have never received a shilling from America since the loss of my dear grandfather—almost the whole of my property is leased which yields but a very small interest."[44] Her desperation often took rather dramatic turns, as she once declared to West, about their joint investment, "If the Road does not succeed, I shall be sent to Bedlam."[45]

Exactly when the pneumatic railway's bubble burst is unclear. However, it would seem to have occurred in 1837, for that is when the Marquess of Wellesley was found insolvent. He was then provided with a trust of twenty thousand

BALTIMORE, lithograph by Philip Haas, 1837. Library of Congress.

pounds administered by a group of financiers from Leadenhall Street in the City. It was also in the summer of that year that West left England for New York, and then Baltimore. He was bankrupt, and had placed his possessions in the hands of Colonel Thomas Aspinwall, United States Consul in London. Apparently he had secured whatever loan had been necessary for his passage to America. Rumors abounded that his health was broken, and his fortunes ruined.

West's arrival in Baltimore may be loosely dated by a letter sent to him from Aaron Vail in New York. "It is only within two days that I have heard from our friend, Irving, what corner of the habitable globe you were likely to be found in." [46] West had undoubtedly left London as discreetly as possible, not to avoid financial embarrassment, for all his dealings in clearing up the debts he had incurred while there were honest and open, but to avoid a kind of social embarrassment to which he would have been especially vulnerable.

Vail's letter notes that he has learned from Washington Irving that West "had gone to Baltimore with Mr. McLane, to whose care this is addressed." Louis McLane was returning from negotiating several delicate diplomatic matters between Great Britain and the United States. West had met him in London.

West's choice of Baltimore as a place to rebuild his fortune and repay his debts was a clever and well-chosen move. His connection with the Patterson and Caton families gave him access to the old Baltimore ascendancy, the merchant princes who played such a large part in the city's prosperity. Louis McLane, a man of great influence and president of a successful railroad, would have been able to give him introductions to the newer generation in Baltimore.

As early as November 1837, Colonel Aspinwall wrote to West to clarify that "out of your remittance I have paid to our friends March and Bates £25 each," indicating that West immediately began to pay his debts and loans.[47] By the summer of 1838, he had established a studio on Baltimore Street, and the *Baltimore Monument,* a local journal "dedicated to the arts and literature," felt that "We should be doing ourselves injustice were we not to mention with marked distinction the highly finished and exquisitely conceived pictures of Mr. West whose room is on Baltimore Street and at this time contains many likenesses of our most distinguished citizens."[48]

West would, indeed, number among his sitters many of the most distinguished citizens of Baltimore, for in addition to the McLane family he painted Robert E. Lee, the politician Reverdy Johnson, a member of the Gilmor family whose art collection was the most substantial in antebellum America, and a number of people from the mercantile and professional classes.

In January of 1839, he had been able to write to Colonel Aspinwall in England, *I have deferred writing you till now that I might speak with the more certainty of my affairs and prospects. At present I think I may venture to say that they are flattering beyond what I could have hoped, and before one year passes over my head, I shall have paid every cent I owe and have a considerable surplus in the bargain.*[49]

This does not seem to be the usual piece of West exaggeration. An accounting of his portrait commissions in the years 1837–1841 indicates the largest known quantity of his work. Still, he had left behind a great deal in London. Concerning paintings left with his old landlord at 15 Wigmore Street, he says in his same letter to Colonel Aspinwall, "tell him not to sell the paintings I left with him," and inquires after two paintings left with his framer, a Mr. Thomas, one of which was the genre picture *The Toilet.*

Colonel Aspinwall, in his response, was "delighted to have so exhilarating a letter from you," and conveyed the message that the landlord and Mr. Thomas had "Everything, in their keeping, exactly as you left it."[50] All those to whom West was responsible were willing to defer interest on the amount owed, which he nevertheless insisted on paying; and those who held his personal property kept it safe pending his instructions. The large history picture *Judith,* the portrait of Felicia Hemans and *The Muses of Painting, Poetry, and Music* are among the pictures which were returned to West and remained in his possession until he died. But there is no mention, in any of the accounts by West's nieces and nephews, that other personal items of furniture or books came with him to Nashville near the end of his life, when he took up residence in a room at his sister's home.

Perhaps this great financial disaster provoked West's most productive period, a period when his most substantial work was accomplished. A strong Protestant

JUDITH, by William Edward West, oil on canvas, not dated. Unlocated. Reproduced in *Putnam's Monthly*, September 1907. Archives of American Art, Smithsonian Institution.

frontier background, combined with a middle-class concern over status and a romantic notion of the artist's role in society may have pushed West into this great moment of maturity and creativity.

While many of the portraits from the Baltimore period repeat certain formulas, all have a highly finished quality, rendering them distinct from the body of contemporary portraiture. During his sojourn in Europe, West seems to have learned to glaze and model the sitters' features into a smooth, rounded, well-controlled expression, while capturing some of the character of the individual.

He was successful with both male and female characterizations. The portraits of Reverdy Johnson and Robert E. Lee demonstrate a near-uncanny perception. Johnson is seen standing in a three-quarter-length mode, with hands folded over his chest in an attitude of wary deliberation, befitting his status as a lawyer. There is, in the raised eyebrows and the windswept hair, some romantic quality either real or idealized about this highly successful son of old Maryland, referred to by his contemporaries as "a Roman Senator of the elder days."

West's portrait of Robert Edward Lee is undoubtedly his finest portrait of a male sitter, and perhaps his best work. Robert E. Lee, "the handsomest man in the army," had a serene, attractive countenance that might have been difficult to capture.[51] Lee was apparently one of those figures in history whose inner sense of self was reflected by an outward composure and an unalterable dignity. In this first life portrait of him, painted before the trials of secession and civil war, he smiles serenely, stopping just short of smugness or arrogance.

The women who sat to West fared as well, if not better, than his male sitters. The lessons of twenty years abroad, and a virtuoso capacity to capture feminine beauty in standard conventions, created a body of work during the Baltimore phase that is an essay in the style and the manner of portraiture in those last hours before the daguerreotype. Again and again, West seems to have returned to his Italian-inspired painting, *The Muses,* for the conventions used in these portraits.

In many, we find the hair smoothly parted in the middle, one strand on the right side just beginning to separate from the rest of the solid mass and slip towards the eye. The small vase of flowers returns, to be placed to the right or the left of the middle of the picture plane, upon some imaginary ledge and perhaps in front of the obligatory piece of drapery.

Some of the ladies appear with corkscrew curls, and all are depicted with large, ample bosoms, beribboned in a fashion reminiscent of the diaphanous gowns of the regency period. Many have necks joined to their bodies by one long, languid line from nape to shoulder, the old, familiar, baroque ogee curve disguised as human flesh. All are glamorized, even the rather plain *Mary Ann Randolph Custis Lee.*

West painted young brides, recent mothers, and older society matrons in their full maturity . The portrait of Mrs. William Duncan McKim [Cat. no. 32] is an interesting study of the benign—that power of portraiture to convey a reflective sensibility, the small, composed expression that would be the prize of the drawing room.

The New York City Directory for 1841 lists William Edward West's address as 8 Bond Street and his occupation as painter. We can assume that he had repaid his bills by that time. His residence in the heart of the financial district of old New York confirms Colonel Aspinwall's earlier prediction that "the time would come, when you would be anxiously enquiring 'what is the price of stocks today', and making thrifty investments of your semi-annual dividends."[52] The Colonel's admonition—"I trust you will not again stumble upon a Pneumatic Railway"—seems to have been well taken. He further offers, "The brush and the palette are good steady old friends, and you must never turn your back upon them."

Though William Edward West did not turn his back upon painting in the last years remaining in his life, he was not as productive as he had been during his Baltimore phase, returning instead to his old pattern of dallying in the homes of the wealthy and painting several family members during the course of his stay. He became closely associated with the W. H. Astor family, and painted several Astor portraits.

One of his sitters, during the New York period, was the merchant Warren Delano, the grandfather of Franklin Roosevelt, who would later write to West

REVERDY JOHNSON, by William Edward West, oil on canvas, circa 1838–1841. The Maryland Historical Society, Baltimore, Maryland. [Cat. no. 28]

ROBERT E. LEE, by William Edward West, oil on canvas, 1838. Washington and Lee University, Lexington, Virginia. [Cat. no. 31]

MARY ANN RANDOLPH CUSTIS LEE, by William Edward West, oil on canvas, 1838. Washington and Lee University, Lexington, Virginia. [Cat. no. 30]

NEW YORK CITY, view from St. Paul's Church, by Henry Papprill after J. W. Hill, aquatint, 1849. Print Collection, The New York Public Library, Astor, Lenox, and Tilden Foundations.

in Nashville, assuring him that he had "friends in New York who will have much pleasure in hearing from you—and the more so if they can hear of your continued good health—and your enjoyment of the scenes of your early life"—indicating that West may have dined out often on the episode of painting Lord Byron.[53]

His connection with Irving, who was American Minister to Spain from 1842 to 1846, was still helpful. Through Irving, West met and painted the writer William Gilmore Simms and the historian William H. Prescott. West frequently visited Irving at Sunnyside, and accompanied him, on several occasions, to Boston.

West had already illustrated several paintings based on stories by Washington Irving and, during this period, several of them, including *The Pride of the Village* and *Annette Delarbre,* were engraved by Joseph Andrews and enjoyed a wide circulation.[54] Several of his other paintings in allegorical or genre modes were engraved as well, especially his *Cupid and Psyche,* which Henry Tuckerman mentions having seen in 1849.

In an article on West which Tuckerman published in *Literary Life* of April 1849, he mentions a trip to West's studio where he saw "a cabinet-size work." [55] This is a reference to the "cabinet" or "fancy" pictures West is supposed to have painted during this last phase of his life. In these paintings, mythological or fanciful themes and settings are used to render the sitter in a more cultivated fashion. Tuckerman's observation that West was "doubtless the best example

New York, August 7th 1849.

M. E. West, Esq

Sir,

I am instructed by the Executive Committee to make you an offer of $650 for your two paintings framed. Viz: "Cupid & Psyche" and "The Present" payable by draft on the Treasurer at 4 months. Please advise at your earliest convenience whether the offer is accepted.

Respectfully yours

Andrew Warner
Cor. Sey.

Painted by W. E. West.   Engraved by W Humphrys.

CUPID AND PSYCHE.

AMERICAN ART UNION bill of sale for *Cupid and Psyche* and *The Present* by William Edward West, dated August 7, 1849. William Edward West Papers, Archives of American Art, Smithsonian Institution.

CUPID AND PSYCHE, by William Humphreys after William Edward West, engraving, not dated. Print Collection, The New York Public Library, Astor, Lenox, and Tilden Foundations.

ELIZABETH HENRIETTA YOUNG AND ANNA ELIZABETH MERCER, by William Edward West, oil on canvas, circa 1852. William Barrow Floyd. [Cat. no. 45]

among us of the English School" refers to his associations with Leslie, Wilkie, and other English genre painters of the early nineteenth century. Tuckerman found West to be "an ardent lover of Wilkie, Leslie and Newton," whose work, especially Wilkie's *The Blind Fiddler*, enjoyed a great popularity in this country in its engraved form.

One of the pictures Tuckerman saw during that visit was *The Present*, which West had painted some years earlier and had exhibited at the Royal Academy.

Another reference is to a young girl in Greek costume, again executed at an earlier period. So it seems likely that if West was "excelling at fancy cabinet pictures," it was an excellence culled from extant painting and not work in progress.

The only painting which exists from that last period, which might fall into the category of "fancy cabinet painting," is the portrait of Miss E. H. Young and her youthful companion, Miss Anna Mercer. That picture, which returns West, late in life, to a Natchez subject, is a curiously compressed painting of two figures seated side by side, in a fully furnished room. The figure on the left, Miss Young, is dressed entirely in black, suggesting mourning, while the figure on the right, Miss Mercer, is clad entirely in white, a sepulchral expression upon her face, her hand reaching out. Correspondence with West from Miss Young suggests that one of the likenesses was done from a daguerreotype. The painting has the air of a Victorian mourning painting, the dark and somewhat somber background relieved by the colorful furnishings and the stark contrast of the costumes.

Tuckerman observed that West mingled "little with younger artists, but was the favored guest of a few attached families, until the infirmities of age induced his return to his nearest living kindred at Nashville, Tennessee." [56] In 1855 his sister, Jane West Woods, in a letter announcing West's impending arrival, discloses, "he says his goods are all packed and he is ready at any time we will name the day." [57] West had been ill with some affliction of the toe, which was "getting better under the present treatment."

William Edward West's last years were spent among his family in Nashville, painting portraits of his young nieces, and telling stories of life in Europe and among the notables of America. He loved to tease his nieces, writing to one, *The flowers are all right—The money is all wrong—one dollar paid for all three tickets—therefore you must do a sum in division and divide a dollar into three parts and when I see you next give me one third and then if we are not even it will be odd (old tricks).*[58]

Once in Nashville, he maintained close ties with various Astors, Delanos, Van Rensselaers, and Schuylers who made up the glittering crowds of New York in the days before the Four Hundred and the robber barons. They would write him long and affectionate letters, expressing apparently sincere regret at his absence from New York, and he would respond with news of "the West"— Nashville and the Tennessee area. The banker Charles Augustus Davis writes concerning his health. Davis had a large accumulation of letters received from the great, which he is about to destroy: "I have hundreds of letters from Clay-Biddle-Adams-Calhoun . . . but as those letters were mostly confidential—though they would make an amusing book, they will a bright bonfire." [59]

In his last years, with increasingly failing health, West began to talk of "spiritualism," and to write to his various friends about being healed. Spiritualism had been the rage in New York for several years during his residence there, as a result of the lectures, writings, and appearances of Andrew Jackson Davis. Davis delivered a series of lectures in Manhattan, which were transcribed and published in 1847 as *Principles of Nature, the Divine Revelations, and a Voice to Mankind.*

NASHVILLE, by an unidentified artist, lithograph, 1849–1851. Print Collection, The New York Public Library, Astor, Lenox, and Tilden Foundations.

Mary Van Rensselaer, writing to West, felt that reading Davis's work "brought you right before me as we sat that last evening at Mrs. Vail's and you told me the delight you had experienced in reading of the Celestial Spheres." Gratified that West was seeking salvation and healing outside this world and the world of art, she "felt that our heavenly Father had in his love spoken to you, and it did not become me to question the medium through which your immortal nature had been approached." [60]

His friend Charles Augustus Davis took a slightly different view. He told West, "a good old lady not long since was enquired of by a wellknown devine here why she went and offered herself every time confirmation was held, to be confirmed—'Well,' says she, 'I was told and I find it true—that it is good for the rheumatiz'." [61]

West must have thought so as well, regarding spiritualism, for by April of 1857 he was writing to Margaret Astor that he was in "a sad state of body and mind" and was "going to try spiritual power, though, I am obliged to do it by correspondence—I have more faith in the healing mediums when the patient is present, than in all the Doctors—this is my last resource—if it fails-why then-Good-night." [62] His health prevented him from accepting an invitation to winter in Natchez with the Edward Turner family.

Despite the productivity of his first days during the Nashville reconnoiter, his last months were unproductive and depressing. "Alas, I have not taken my brush in my hand for five months—and what is life worth with nothing to do but to suffer and think of happier by-gone hours," he writes to Margaret Astor in the same letter. However, this fatalistic remark did not prevent him from inquiring about friends and affairs in New York. "There is not a line that is not interesting to me."

Mrs. Astor responded immediately with a newsy letter. She must have sensed that West's life was coming to an end, for she closes her letter with "Good bye, my dear Mr. West, I pray that God may bless you for time and eternity." [63]

William Edward West died on November 2, 1857, and is buried with his family in the old city cemetery in Nashville, Tennessee.

NOTES

1. Mabel Van Dyke Baer, "The Ancestry of Edward West," *The Register of the Kentucky Historical Society* 58, no. 4 (October 1960) : 354–62.

2. For a discussion of Edward West's life and work, see Margaret M. Bridwell, "Edward West, Silversmith and Inventor," *The Filson Club History Quarterly* 21 (1947) : 301 *et seq.*; and Margaret M. Bridwell, "Three Early Kentucky Silversmiths," *Antiques* 78, no. 6 (December 1960) : 579 *et seq.*

3. See Thomas D. Clark, *A History of Kentucky* (Lexington, Ky., 1960), p. 158. "Kentucky" seems to have meant "dark and bloody ground" in the Indian vernacular.

4. The definitive history of antebellum Kentucky is by Lewis Collins, and was first published as *History of Kentucky* in Maysville, Kentucky, in 1847. The text most often used and reprinted is the edition by his son, Richard, which brings events up to 1874. That volume, *Collins's History of Kentucky,* was reprinted in Louisville, Kentucky, in 1924; and the quotation cited here is found on page 169.

5. Edna Talbott Whitley, *Kentucky Ante-Bellum Portraiture,* The National Society of the Colonial Dames of America in the Commonwealth of Kentucky (Richmond, Va., 1956) , pp. 775–78.

6. Marion Mulligan Ross, "Story of West, Painter . . .," *Lexington* (Kentucky) *Leader,* May 1, 1921, Sunday supplement (unpaged). Mrs. Ross lived in Lexington, and had access to materials on West in the University of Kentucky library. She also quotes extensively from Nellie Porterfield Dunn's article "An Artist of the Past: William Edward West and His Friends at Home and Abroad" in the September 1907 *Putnam's Monthly* magazine. She was in correspondence with West's niece Aduella Norvell Bryant, and quotes from material that Mrs. Bryant sent to her.

7. Both the Ross and Dunn articles cite Dr. Samuel Brown as the source of West's means to travel to Philadelphia to study with Sully.

8. William Edward West to Thomas Sully, New Orleans, January 28, 1817, Charles Henry Hart Autograph Collection, Archives of American Art, Smithsonian Institution.

9. Cited in Ross, "Story of West, Painter."

10. William Edward West to Jane West Woods, Natchez, December 19, 1818, William Edward West Papers, Archives of American Art, Smithsonian Institution.

11. All quotations from William Edward West's letter to his father, Edward West (Florence, February 4, 1820) , which follow are derived from the text of the same letter, as published in the Nashville *Tennessean.* This clipped article is glued to the inside of West's portfolio of letters and notes now in the Archives of American Art, Smithsonian Institution. Also attached to the portfolio is this notation: "This portfolio containing notes and letters to my mother's bachelor brother, Wm. E. West was given me by his brother, Patterson B. West in 1858—I now give this portfolio with all the said notes and letters to my niece Mrs. Moselle Norvell Elliott." Mrs. Elliott's great-granddaughter, Gertrude Elliott McNabb Meissner, donated the same portfolio to the Archives of American Art.

12. Estill Curtis Pennington, "Painting Lord Byron: An Account by William Edward West," *Archives of American Art Journal* 24, no. 2 (1984), pp. 16–21.

13. William Edward West to Thomas Sully, Florence, January 29, 1820. Pennsylvania Historical Society microfilm project, Archives of American Art, Smithsonian Institution. All subsequent quotations addressed to Sully are from the same letter. Also reproduced in Whitley, *Kentucky Ante-Bellum Portraiture,* pp. 776–77.

14. Joel Tanner Hart (1810–1877) was born in Winchester, Kentucky, and lived and worked in Florence from 1848 to 1877. He is best known for his portrait busts and idealized figures in the manner of Hiram Powers.

15. William Edward West's handwritten account of his encounter with Lord Byron is in the William Edward West Papers, Archives of

American Art, Smithsonian Institution. Substantially the same text was published in the *New Monthly Magazine and Literary Journal*, part 1 (Original papers) (London, 1826). A full discussion of the West-Byron encounter appears with the published text of West's account in Estill Curtis Pennington, "Painting Lord Byron: An Account by West," pp. 16–21.

16. George Noel Gordon, Lord Byron, *The Works of Lord Byron: Letters and Journals*, edited by R. E. Prothero, vol. 6 (1898; reprint London, 1904), p. 73.

17. The "Carbonari" was a secret society that believed Jesus Christ was the ultimate victim of the type of tyranny they opposed. In July 1820, they rose in revolt in the Southern Kingdom of the Two Sicilies, attempting to overthrow the House of Savoy and install a more liberal parliamentary government. Their activities prefigured Garibaldi's unification efforts.

18. Cited in Pennington, "Painting Byron: West's Account," pp. 16–21.

19. In Canto 8, lines 61–67. The preferred edition of *Don Juan* is found in Frederick Page, ed., *Byron's Poetical Works*, 3rd edition, corrected by John Jump (London, 1970). See John Clubbe, *Byron's Natural Man: Daniel Boone and Kentucky* (Lexington, Ky., 1979) *passim*. Clubbe discusses West's possible suggestion of Daniel Boone to Byron in this book and in his article, "William Edward West's Portrait of Teresa Guiccioli," in the 1979 *Byron Journal*, pp. 76–87.

20. Washington Irving, in his journals and notebooks, makes frequent mention of the various Bonapartes. Considering the size of the American community abroad, it seems likely that Irving provided West with an introduction to Betsy Bonaparte. At any rate, West painted several members of her family.

21. Washington Irving, *Washington Irving, Journals and Notebooks,* ed. Walter Reichart, vol. 3 (1819–1827), (Madison, Wis., 1970), p. 436.

22. The best account I have read of the visits between West and Irving in Paris is found in George S. Hellman, *Washington Irving Esquire* (New York, 1925), p. 83. Mr. Hellman edited Irving's journals.

23. Washington Irving, *Journals and Notebooks*, vol. 3, p. 482.

24. Washington Irving to William Edward West, Paris, July 15, 1825, William Edward West Papers, Archives of American Art, Smithsonian Institution.

25. Peter Irving (1771–1838) was Washington Irving's brother and also a writer, as well as a financier (see the *Dictionary of American Biography*, vol. 9).

26. Charles Robert Leslie (1794–1859), an Anglo-American history, genre, and portrait painter, was born in London of American parents, and lived briefly in America, but spent most of his life in England. He is best known for his large, romantic depictions of important events in English history.

27. David Wilkie (1785–1841), an English painter, is best known for his history paintings based on important events in English political life. His painting *The Blind Fiddler* was much admired in this country.

28. "In the autumn of 1827 Mr. Alaric Watts, who was then forming a gallery of portraits of living authors of Great Britain, prevailed on Mrs. Hemans to sit for her picture. Mr. West was the artist chosen" (Nellie Porterfield Dunn, unpublished manuscript containing notes and miscellaneous biographical details on William Edward West, Tennessee State Library, Nashville, Tennessee).

29. Felicia Hemans to William Edward West, undated, William Edward West Papers, Archives of American Art, Smithsonian Institution.

30. W. M. Rosetti, ed., *The Poetical Work of Mrs. Felicia Hemans* (New York and Boston, undated), p. 14 (prefatory notice).

31. Rosetti, ed. *Poetical Works of Mrs. Hemans*, p. 14.

32. Felicia Hemans to William Edward West, Dublin, 1831, William Edward West Papers, Archives of American Art, Smithsonian Institution.

33. Felicia Hemans to William Edward West, Dublin, 1831, William Edward West Papers, Archives of American Art, Smithsonian Institution.

34. Felicia Hemans to William Edward West, Dublin, 1831, William Edward West Papers, Archives of American Art, Smithsonian Institution.

35. Charles Henry Hart to Mrs. Benjamin Thaw, Philadelphia, October 1, 1915, Charles Henry Hart Papers, Archives of American Art, Smithsonian Institution.

36. Felicia Hemans to William Edward West, undated, William Edward West Papers, Archives of American Art, Smithsonian Institution.

37. For a discussion of the Southern cotton economy and its relationship to the national economy here and abroad, see Charles S. Sydnor, *The Development of Southern Sectionalism*, vol. 5, History of the South series (Baton Rouge, 1948), pp. 1–32.

38. Mary Caton Patterson Wellesley to William Edward West, Phoenix Park, September 14, 1834, William Edward West Papers, Archives of American Art, Smithsonian Institution. The extensive correspondence between West and the Caton sisters covers the period 1824–1837.

39. William Dunlap, *History of the Rise and Progress of the Arts of Design in the United States*, vol. 2, pt. 1 (1834; reprinted, New York, 1969, p. 271. Dunlap drew most of his comments on West from a letter written to him by Charles Robert Leslie.

40. Elizabeth Caton to William Edward West, Dublin, October 16, 1825, William Edward West Papers, Archives of American Art, Smithsonian Institution.

41. Elizabeth Caton to William Edward West, Dublin, October 16, 1825, William Edward West Papers, Archives of American Art, Smithsonian Institution.

42. Mary Caton Patterson Wellesley to William Edward West, Phoenix Park, September 14, 1833, William Edward West Papers, Archives of American Art, Smithsonian Institution.

43. Washington Irving, *Letters*, vol. 2 (1823–1839), edited by Ralph M. Aderman, *et al.* (Boston, 1979), p. 482.

44. Elizabeth Caton to William Edward West, Mars Lodge, September 13, 183-?, William Edward West Papers, Archives of American Art, Smithsonian Institution.

45. Elizabeth Caton to William Edward West, undated note, William Edward West Papers, Archives of American Art, Smithsonian Institution.

46. Aaron Vail to William Edward West, Astor House, New York, New York, September 27, 1837, William Edward West Papers, Archives of American Art, Smithsonian Institution.

47. Colonel Thomas Aspinwall to William Edward West, London, November 1837, William Edward West Papers, Archives of American Art, Smithsonian Institution.

48. *Baltimore Monument* 2, no. 43 (July 28, 1838) : 343.

49. William Edward West to Thomas Aspinwall, Baltimore, January 1839, William Edward West Papers, Archives of American Art, Smithsonian Institution.

50. Thomas Aspinwall to William Edward West, London, August 30, 1839, William Edward West Papers, Archives of American Art, Smithsonian Institution.

51. Douglas Southall Freeman, *R. E. Lee,* vol. 1 (New York, 1940) , p. 148.

52. Colonel Thomas Aspinwall to William Edward West, London, August 30, 1839, William Edward West Papers, Archives of American Art, Smithsonian Institution.

53. Warren Delano to William Edward West, New York, April 15, 1856, William Edward West Papers, Archives of American Art, Smithsonian Institution.

54. Joseph Andrews (circa 1805–1873) , a wood- and line-engraver, who worked in Boston producing prints of well-known works of art for mass consumption.

55. There is some confusion concerning the terms "cabinet" and "fancy" pictures when referring to West's work. A "cabinet" portrait is a small picture, usually in the 25.4 x 20.3 cm. (10 x 8 in.) format. A "fancy" picture is a portrait of any size with the subject in some historical garb or setting.

56. Henry T. Tuckerman, *Book of the Artists, American Artist Life* (1867; reprint New York, 1966) , p. 201. An undated letter from Henry Tuckerman in the West Papers (Archives of American Art) extends his regret at not being able to come and visit West at the home of Warren Delano due to ill health.

57. Jane West Woods to Aduella Norvell Bryant, Philadelphia, October 21, 1855, William Edward West Papers, Archives of American Art, Smithsonian Institution. West apparently had his belongings in several places, for as late as 1851 Colonel Aspinwall wrote to him in Boston about property still left behind in England, including one portrait of Felicia Hemans, furniture, and books.

58. William Edward West to "Miss Aleda," Nashville, 1856, William Edward West Papers, Archives of American Art, Smithsonian Institution.

59. Charles Augustus Davis to William Edward West, New York, February 12, 1856, William Edward West Papers, Archives of American Art, Smithsonian Institution.

60. Mary Van Rensselaer to William Edward West, Dresden, May 4, 1856, William Edward West Papers, Archives of American Art, Smithsonian Institution. The wife of Phillip Van Rensselaer, United States Counsel to Dresden, Mary Van Rensselaer kept up a large correspondence with West, acquainting him with the activities of friends from his European days who continued to serve in the diplomatic corps, most notably Aaron Vail and Thomas Aspinwall. This particular epistle—full of chatty gossip about European nobility, the sights, sounds, and smells of Dresden, and her own family adventures—runs to more than twenty pages!

61. Charles Augustus Davis to William Edward West, February 12, 1856, No. 1 University Place, New York, New York, William Edward West Papers, Archives of American Art, Smithsonian Institution.

62. William Edward West to Margaret Astor, Nashville, April 2, 1857, William Edward West Papers, Archives of American Art, Smithsonian Institution.

63. Margaret Astor to William Edward West, undated (1857) , William Edward West Papers Archives of American Art, Smithsonian Institution.

Catalogue of the Exhibition

1.

Edward West, Jr.

1757–1827

Oil on canvas, 73.7 x 58.4 cm. (29 x 23 in.)
Circa 1805
Source of attribution: family documentation
Nell Foster Waltz

Edward West, Jr., tinker, silversmith, gunmaker, and inventor, was the son of Edward and Elizabeth Mills West of Stafford County, Virginia. In 1784 Edward West, Sr., settled in Georgetown, Scott County, Kentucky, where his son followed him a year later. Edward West, Jr., held eight land grants in Kentucky when it was still a province of Virginia. He is cited as a landholder in Bourbon County in the *First Census of Kentucky* (1790). He married Sarah Brown, the daughter of Samuel and Maria Creed Brown, before moving to Lexington.

There is considerable confusion in existing texts concerning his parentage and his association with the Brown family, which affected attributions of kinship to his son William Edward West. Edward West was not the son of Dr. William West of St. Paul's Church, Baltimore; nor was he related to the artist Benjamin West. Nor was Dr. Samuel Brown his father-in-law.

Edward West invented a steamboat device that plied Elkhorn Creek in Fayette County, Kentucky, and he patented a device for cutting nails. He was also a silversmith of note, although he did not often sign his silver. He had a shop on High Street in Lexington. His work was greatly admired by his contemporaries. Samuel McCullough, who owned miniatures by West's sons John B. and William E., found him a man "of all work, all ideas. He could make a watch or a clock, or he could mend one. He could make a rifle or a gun, or he could mend one, within my recollection he could make or mend anything."

Edward and Sarah West had twelve children. This portrait has descended through the family of Sarah Brown West, who in 1818 married Robert Woods of Nashville. It is currently owned by a descendant. William Edward West's parents died while he was abroad. They are buried in the old Presbyterian Cemetery in Lexington.

2.

Dr. Samuel Brown

1769–1830

Oil on canvas, 83.8 x 71.1 cm. (33 x 28 in.)

Circa 1807

Source of attribution: family documentation

The University of Kentucky Art Museum,
Lexington, Kentucky

Samuel Brown was one of four Brown brothers, sons of John and Margaret Preston Brown, who were important figures in the development of Kentucky from a frontier province of Virginia into the fifteenth state of the Union. Samuel Brown was trained as a doctor in Scotland, taking a degree from the University of Aberdeen, one of the leading medical schools of that day. He is credited with introducing a vaccine for smallpox into the Lexington community in 1802, and with establishing a medical school at Transylvania University in Lexington, the first school of higher learning west of the Alleghenies.

Brown lived in Lexington from 1797 until 1806. It was then that he made contact with William Edward West's father, with whom he shared an interest in scientific experimentation. Brown is mentioned in several texts of that period as a source of funds for William Edward West's travel to Italy in 1819. It seems certain that Dr. Brown provided West with many of his contacts in the lower Mississippi River valley, as he lived in New Orleans from 1806 until 1809, when he married Catherine Percy from Natchez, Mississippi. West mentions Dr. Brown in one of the extant letters from his Florentine period.

Samuel Brown died following an attack of apoplexy at the home of his brother-in-law, in Huntsville, Alabama. Dr. Brown's portrait hangs at the University of Kentucky Medical Center Library, commemorating his contributions to the early medical history of Kentucky.

3.

Michael Gratz

1740–1811

Pastel on paper, 60.9 x 50.8 cm. (24 x 20 in.)
Circa 1809
Signed, lower left: "W.E.W."
National Portrait Gallery, Smithsonian Institution

Michael Gratz was a native of Upper Silesia in what is now East Germany. Following various business adventures in Europe and Great Britain, he spent one year in India, in an effort to establish himself as a merchant. When this did not work out, he joined his brother Barnard in Philadelphia, and there they formed a business and trading partnership which plied the coastal trade routes from Quebec to New Orleans. They eventually operated a steamboat company that made the journey from Pittsburgh to Cincinnati and on into the Indiana Territory. Michael Gratz was a patriot, and took the oath of allegiance to Virginia in 1783. He had extensive landholdings in the Western territory, especially Kentucky, where a large part of his family removed at the time of the founding of Lexington. Gratz Park was named in their honor.

Michael Gratz was the father of the philanthropist Rebecca, who was also a West subject. The family provided extensive connections for West, and it may have been through their auspices that he became acquainted with both Thomas Sully and Washington Irving. Irving's fiancée, Matilda Hoffman, was a close friend of Rebecca Gratz, who nursed her through her final illness.

This pastel drawing of Michael Gratz bears West's monogram, and is the only example of a West pastel still known to exist.

4.

Julien de Lallande Poydras

1740–1824

Oil on canvas, 88.9 x 71.1 cm. (35 x 28 in.)

Circa 1817

Source of attribution: minutes of the Female Orphan
Society of New Orleans, June 15, 1817

Poydras Home,
New Orleans, Louisiana

Born in the French province of Brittany, Julien de Lallande Poydras immigrated to New Orleans in 1768, and became one of the wealthiest men in the Louisiana Territory. His first efforts in being a peddler in the lower Mississippi River valley were apparently successful, for in 1789 he had a large trading post and plantation at the Pointe Coupée Parish, Louisiana, which became his principal residence for the rest of his life. Monsieur Poydras was also an ambitious poet, who penned a paean to the Louisiana victory over the French at Baton Rouge in 1779, entitled *La Prise du Morne du Baton Rouge*. A subsequent literary critic, E. L. Tinker, described Poydras's poetry as "A hard-worked pony ballet of nymphs." A close friend of territorial Governor William Claiborne in the days after the Louisiana Purchase, Poydras held several posts in the territorial, and later state, governments. He was President of the Constitutional Convention of 1812, and a presidential elector in the same year. He was twice president of the Louisiana State Senate: 1812–1813 and 1820–1821.

Poydras's greatest contribution to posterity, however, was his philanthropic legacy. He founded and endowed the Poydras Female Orphan Asylum, which still operates as the Poydras Home. The minutes of this organization note the gift of Poydras's portrait as "a masterly production . . . from the pencil of Mr. West." Poydras left a legacy to provide dowries for indigent brides in the Pointe Coupée and West Baton Rouge parishes, which still makes bequests. He remained a bachelor; Poydras Street in the business district of New Orleans is named in his honor.

5.

Catherine Surget Bingaman

1776–1841

Oil on canvas, 91.5 x 71.1 cm. (36 x 28 in.)

Circa 1818

Source of attribution: correspondence in William Edward West Papers, Archives of American Art, Smithsonian Institution

Linton Surget Collection, Tulane University Art Collection, New Orleans, Louisiana

While ill from the yellow fever in 1818, West resided with the Bingaman family at their plantation, Fatherland, four miles from Natchez, Mississippi. He found Catherine Surget Bingaman and her family to be "my most particular friends," and felt her to be "the finest and first woman in the county."

The daughter of Pierre and Katrina Surget, Catherine Surget grew up at Cherry Grove Plantation. Mr. Surget had made a fortune trading in the lower Mississippi River valley, sometimes under circumstances to which he jokingly referred as "pirating." The Surgets were something of a golden clan in Natchez in the days when that wild town on the Mississippi was the leading city north of New Orleans. Mrs. Bingaman's son Adam earned quite a reputation as a local personality, often being referred to as "our Lord Byron."

William Edward West felt he had received such an abundance of kindness from them that he "could talk about them forever," and the Surgets and Bingamans figured often in his tales of Mississippi and Louisiana.

6.

John Tucker Bowdoin

1787–1821

Oil on canvas, 76.2 x 63.5 cm. (30 x 25 in.)
Circa 1818
Label on reverse of painting reads: "West pinxit"
John Page Elliott

John Tucker Bowdoin was the descendant of the French Huguenot family Baudouin, whose first American representative landed at Pasco Bay, Maine. The Bowdoins were influential in the colonial history of Maine and Massachusetts, and Bowdoin College is named for the family. John Tucker Bowdoin was a wealthy merchant and farmer, the son of Preeson and Courtney Tucker Bowdoin. In 1813 he married Sally Edwards Browne of Four Mile Tree Farm in Surrey County, Virginia, and took up residence there on her family property. Mrs. Bowdoin died two years later.

Bowdoin was well educated, and traveled extensively in Europe. He was noted in his family for his collection of rare books and prints. While on business to Philadelphia, he died in the boardinghouse of Mrs. Fullerton. As he was frequently in Philadelphia, it is likely that the portrait was painted there.

59

7.

Joseph Emery Davis

1784–1870

Oil on canvas, 68.6 x 55.9 cm. (27 x 22 in.)

Circa 1818

Source of attribution: family documentation

Percival T. Beacroft, Jr., Rosemont Plantation,
Woodville, Mississippi

Joseph Emery Davis was the eldest son of the ten children of Samuel and Jane Cook Davis, whose youngest son, Jefferson, would become President of the Confederate States of America. Joseph Davis was born in Augusta, Georgia, but moved at the age of twelve to Christian County, Kentucky, to live on land his father had received as a Revolutionary War land grant. Davis studied law with a Judge Wallace of Russellville, Kentucky, before the family moved to Wilkinson County, Mississippi, in 1811. When Samuel Davis died in 1824, Joseph Davis undertook the care and education of his younger brother Jefferson, enrolling him in the United States Military Academy at West Point. In 1827 Davis gave up his law practice to assume the life of a Mississippi planter at his plantation, The Hurricane, in Warren County, eighteen miles from Natchez.

At the time of the War Between the States, Joseph Davis, who had no interest in a Southern nation, attempted to maintain neutrality. But on June 24, 1862, Union forces advancing on Vicksburg under the command of General Peter J. Osterhaus occupied The Hurricane and gave the family thirty minutes to abandon the house and their private property. The house was then burned to the ground, the contents of the library providing the kindling. This portrait was among the few personal belongings to survive the conflagration.

Jefferson Davis, in a letter to Mary Lucinda Hamer, great-granddaughter of Joseph Davis, dated January 17, 1889, attributes the portrait to West. The freshness of the painted jabot and the sparsity of background detail rival Gilbert Stuart in neoclassical elegance.

61

8.

Joseph Dunbar

1783–1846

Oil on canvas, 72.7 x 60 cm. (28⅝ x 23⅝ in.)

Circa 1818

Source of attribution: research by Sara Lewis Flanary
("William Edward West in New Orleans and Mississippi,"
Antiques 124, no. 5 [November 1983]: 1010 *ff.*)

Caroline Shields Sessions

Joseph Dunbar was the son of Robert Dunbar of Oakley Grove Plantation, Natchez, Mississippi. The Dunbars were Scottish gentry and among the first settlers in the rich and fertile Natchez district. Joseph Dunbar himself was a successful planter. According to a contemporary account, Dunbar had "600 acres in cultivation, and works fifty field hands, and 40 horses and mules, and ten yokes of oxen." There were more than 150 slaves on the Dunbar plantation, who lived in quarters Robinson thought "as neat as a New England village." The plantation had a steam sawmill, and tobacco, as well as cotton, was cultivated.

9.

Olivia Magruder Dunbar

1786–1853

Oil on canvas, 70.2 x 60 cm. (25⅝ x 23⅝ in.)

Circa 1818

Source of attribution: research by Sara Lewis Flanary
("William Edward West in New Orleans and Mississippi,"
Antiques 124, no. 5 [November 1983]: 1010 *ff.*)

Caroline Shields Sessions

The wife of Joseph Dunbar, Olivia Magruder was found to "take pride in showing . . . her neat dairy room, and long rows of barrels of sweetest lard, best tallow and two year old soap, all prepared and put up under her own personal supervision." The Dunbars had no children, but the portraits have remained in the family through lateral descent.

10.

John Richards

1787–1827

Oil on canvas, 90.2 x 69.8 cm. (35½ x 27½ in.)
Circa 1818
Source of attribution: author's examination
State Historical Museum, Mississippi Department of
Archives and History, Jackson, Mississippi

John Richards, "a younger son of Virginia," moved to Natchez, Mississippi, in
1807 and became a successful cotton merchant and commission agent. In 1811 he
married Sarah Buckholtz, and they had one child, who died at an early age. "He lived
in princely style and was a popular bon vivant with a well-filled cellar of fine wines,"
according to a contemporary account. The Natchez papers make mention of his
entertaining cotton merchants from Liverpool. He is thought to have died from bleed-
ing of the gums after having a tooth extracted in 1827. At the time of his death, he
was a probate judge in Natchez. The creases and striations in Richards's suit, as
West has rendered them, have a folk-art quality.

11.

Sarah Buckholtz Richards

1792–1886

Oil on canvas, 90.2 x 69.8 cm. (35½ x 27½ in.)

Circa 1818

State Historical Museum, Mississippi Department of
Archives and History, Jackson, Mississippi

Sarah Buckholtz, the eldest daughter of Captain Jacob and Mrs. Sarah Buckholtz, was born in Amite County, Mississippi, in 1792. At the time of her birth, Mississippi was under Spanish rule, and her native county was a part of the old Natchez district. When she married John Richards in 1811, Mississippi had not yet been admitted to the Union, although Natchez was prospering from the cotton commission trade with England in which her husband was involved. After the death of her own child, Sarah Buckholtz Richards attempted to adopt her niece, Sarah Jenkins. Although the parents would not consent, Sarah and John Richards "succeeded in keeping her and had her educated and reared in an affluent style," according to a descendant. She outlived her husband by nearly sixty years, and died in Natchez at the age of ninety-four. Her life spans the growth of Mississippi from frontier territory to statehood, through war and Reconstruction, to renewed peaceful prosperity.

12.

Thomas R. Fosdick

1797–1829

Oil on panel, 66 x 53.3 cm. (26 x 21 in.)
1818
Signed lower left: "West 1818"
Cincinnati Historical Society, Cincinnati, Ohio,
Gift of Frank Johnston Jones

Thomas R. Fosdick emigrated to Cincinnati, Ohio, with his father, Richard Fosdick of New London, Connecticut. He is listed in the 1819 Cincinnati Directory as having an exchange office. He subsequently appears in 1826 as a commission merchant. The close proximity of Lexington to Cincinnati, accentuated by the Ohio River, made the cities natural trading partners. It seems likely that William Edward West painted Fosdick on his way to New Orleans from Philadelphia.

13.

William Edward West

1788–1857

Oil on canvas, 76.2 x 60.9 cm. (30 x 24 in.)

Circa 1819

Source of attribution: William Barrow Floyd, "Portraits
of Ante-Bellum Kentuckians," *Antiques* 105, no. 4
(April 1974) : 808 *ff.*

Private collection

Not in exhibition

The evidence that this work is actually a self-portrait of William Edward West is
purely circumstantial, but convincing. The only other recorded self-portrait of West
appeared with the article by Nellie Porterfield Dunn in the September 1907 *Putnam's
Monthly.* Family correspondence indicates that that second self-portrait was done
sixteen years later, in 1836, while West was in Europe.

There is a distinct physical resemblance between the two portraits, most notably
in the high forehead, the hair brushed on top of the head, the ear on the right side
of the face exposed, and the long sideburns. Most striking is the focus of both
paintings, for, in the classic manner of a self-portrait, the subject is gazing straight
out of the picture plane at the viewer, a direct gaze unlike the coy sidelong glance so
prevalent in West's other work.

The portrait presented here is thought to have been done in Natchez in 1819, and
is similar in style and manner to the other portraits of that period. West's contemporaries, notably Washington Irving, always characterized him as the lively "little"
West. The alert, sprightly expression in this portrait indicates a greater intensity than
that found in his other subjects. The second self-portrait, still in the artist's family,
in a very deteriorated condition, shows a more mature, worldly individual who, after
all, had been traveling in Europe as something of a celebrity for more than fifteen years.

14.

George Noel Gordon, 6th Lord Byron

1788–1824

Oil on canvas, 76.2 x 63.5 cm. (30 x 25 in.)
1822
National Portrait Gallery, Edinburgh, Scotland

The appointment kept between William Edward West and Lord Byron in the summer of 1822 was the greatest single event in the artist's life. The sitting is mentioned in all subsequent accounts of his career, and in his own lifetime it was his chief claim to fame. The first narrative account of the sitting appeared in the *New Monthly Magazine and Literary Journal* of 1826, four years after the portrait sitting, while West was living in England. There are two other accounts of the sitting, one in Henry Tuckerman's *Book of the Artists* (1867), and a handwritten account found among West's papers. All three differ only slightly in approach and incidents, except where a meeting with Leigh Hunt and Percy Shelley is concerned. The original account does not mention Shelley or Hunt. The much later Tuckerman account has West seeing Shelley, Hunt, Byron, the Countess Guiccioli, and her brother all together and laughing in some golden glow following the purported incident of the wounded servant. In the handwritten account, there is only a brief mention of Shelley and Hunt appended to the penultimate paragraph. The duration of the actual sitting and the extent of intimacy achieved between sitter and artist can only be a matter of speculation. From apparent textual evidence, West had several sittings with Lord Byron, many of only one hour, in a two-week period at the end of May, 1822. West wrote in his first account that he went to paint the portrait in July, which cannot be correct. A Byron letter dated Pisa, July 3, 1822, indicates that the sitting ended the previous day.

None of the confusion surrounding the portrait sitting, or who was or was not present, is important to the portrait itself. This confusion does shed a partial light on the character of the artist, however, who was subject to telling tall tales of a Mississippi riverboat quality. They seemed to grow larger and more expansive in the telling, especially in the thirty years between the actual event and the last recorded testimony.

Some have found the portrait an admirable likeness, and it did appear as the frontispiece to an edition of Byron's works published in 1901. Others, like the Countess Guiccioli, did not care for it. The painting enjoys no particular fame as the definitive portrait of Byron today.

15.

Teresa Gamba, Countess Guiccioli

1803–1873

Oil on canvas, 80 x 67.3 cm. (31½ x 26½ in.)
1822
Miami University Art Museum, Miami, Ohio, Gift of
Jonathan S. Bishop

Teresa Gamba met Lord Byron in Venice in 1819, when she was sixteen and married to a man of sixty, Count Guiccioli. When Byron departed for Greece in 1823, she returned to her husband after a four-year dalliance. When the Count died, she married the Marquis de Boissy in 1851, and lived in Florence until the time of her death. She never cared for the portrait of Byron by West, and had little to say about the sitting in *My Recollections of Lord Byron,* published in two volumes in England in 1869.

It would seem that she never saw the portrait of herself by West, who took it with him, as he did the portrait of Lord Byron, when they parted company in the summer of 1822. West offered the *Teresa Guiccioli* to Byron in a letter of September 26, 1822, for fifty dollars. If Byron bought the painting, it was never delivered, for West had it in his possession in England, where it was sold to a private collector in 1829, along with a copy of the Byron portrait.

Teresa Guiccioli was considered, by all who saw her, a beautiful woman, and even West was not satisfied with his result. In September of 1822 he wrote to her of his regret at not having "done more justice to your Ladyship's likeness."

16.

Lord Byron's Visit to the U.S.S. Constitution

Oil on canvas, 30.4 x 40.6 cm. (12 x 16 in.)

Circa 1822-1825

Source of attribution: Kennedy Galleries, New York City, 1965

H. Richard Dietrich, Jr.

Lord Byron, who had a penchant for the unpredictable and the insubordinate, had visited the U.S.S. *Constitution,* a celebrated symbol of freedom and revolution to the Europeans, as it rested in harbor in Leghorn, near his villa at Monte Nero, on May 21, 1822. The visit was particularly successful, as the crew and officers gave Byron a warm and hearty welcome, and he responded in kind. The fanfare did not, however, endear him to the Italian authorities, who were suspicious of his motives, due to his support of revolutionary movements and his liberal inclinations.

The warm feelings for Americans that Byron recognized on this visit, and his growing American public, may have rendered him more receptive to having his portrait painted by West. He had already been contacted by George K. Bruen concerning the sitting, which took place sometime after the visit of the frigate. This is West's only known marine painting.

17.

Leigh Hunt

1784–1859

Oil on canvas, 22.8 x 18.4 cm. (9 x 7¼ in.)

Circa 1824

Reattribution by the author based on extant evidence

Manuscripts Department, The University of Virginia
Library, Charlottesville, Virginia

This cabinet portrait first surfaced in West's estate, and was inherited by his niece, Aduella Price Norvell Bryant. It was Mrs. Bryant who identified the sitter as the poet Percy Bysshe Shelley, and sold it as such to Mrs. Nellie Porterfield Dunn. Mrs. Dunn published it in "Unknown Pictures of Shelley" in the October 1905 issue of *Century* magazine. West, however, made no mention of Shelley in his initial account of the Byron sitting, nor did he exhibit a portrait of Shelley in his lifetime. Newman White, in his biography, *Shelley* (1940), makes a convincing argument that the portrait is actually of Leigh Hunt.

Hunt lived in Florence from 1823 to 1825, as did West. A lesser-known writer of the English Romantic movement, he was closely associated with Byron and Shelley. Hunt returned to England from Italy, and continued writing. He is best known for his fanciful poem, *Abou-ben-Adhem,* and for his critical essays. Hunt outlived his Romantic contemporaries to become a well-known Victorian writer. A much-praised play, *A Legend of Florence,* was a favorite of Queen Victoria's.

18.

Dominick Lynch, Jr.

1786–1857

Oil on canvas, 90.2 x 72.4 cm. (35½ x 28½ in.)
1824–1825
The New-York Historical Society, New York City

Washington Irving mentions seeing Lynch pose for his portrait in West's studio in Paris in late 1824 and early 1825. Lynch was the son of a wealthy New York merchant and staunch Roman Catholic who had founded and built St. Peter's Church on Barclay Street. Dominick Lynch, Jr., contributed to the support of this church, as well as to more secular endeavors, for he is credited with bringing the first Italian Opera Company to New York. He became a lawyer in Rome, New York, a city he helped found.

Two known portraits of Lynch have been credited to William Edward West. The other, in the possession of the Long Island Historical Society, is of a much younger person, and the costume does not fit the period established by the Irving journal entry. This portrait does have a label on the back which reads "painted in Paris in 1821." That date is unlikely, a supposition supported by the date of Irving's journal entry, and by West's presence in Florence until 1824.

Clearly West's interest in Sir Thomas Lawrence affected the composition and pose of this work, distinguished from his earlier work by its far more sophisticated, romantic manner.

19.

The Muses of Painting, Poetry, and Music

Oil on canvas, 95.9 x 83.2 cm. (37¾ x 32¾ in.)

Circa 1825

Source of attribution: family documentation

Corcoran Gallery of Art, Washington, D. C., gift of
Elizabeth H. E. McNabb, in memory of Sarah West
Norvell Leonard

An air of mystery surrounds this fanciful painting. West's subjects may have been the Caton sisters of Baltimore, his great friends and confidantes while he lived in Paris—a possibility suggested by Mrs. McNabb, the descendant of West's sister, Sarah, who gave the painting to the Corcoran. Family tradition maintains that West painted *The Muses* and Lord Byron's portrait in Italy in 1835, but Byron's portrait is known to have been done in 1822. Washington Irving's journals of 1824–1825 mention the Caton sisters sitting to West in Paris. It seems most likely that *The Muses,* with its faint aura of Ingres, was done at that time. Stylistically it is more fully realized than West's early portraiture, but not as accomplished as his English work.

There are no exhibition records to indicate that the painting was ever shown publicly in West's lifetime, but he always kept it in his possession, retrieving it from England in the aftermath of his financial calamity of 1837. The ambitious intention of the painting, a combination of mannerist composition and florid Italiante coloration, indicates West's earnest desire to demonstrate the lessons learned in Florence.

20.

Edward Patterson

1789–1865

Oil on canvas, 76.2 x 63.5 cm. (30 x 25 in.)

Circa 1825

Source of attribution: family documentation

The Maryland Historical Society, Baltimore, Gift of
Mrs. Andrew Robeson

An air of confidence pervades this portrait of the successful Baltimore business-man, Edward Patterson, who gazes out from the picture plane with a shrewd, smug expression.

Edward's father was William Patterson, a strict parent whose "great desire to keep my sons in view induced me to pass them all through my own counting house." This must have proven a good idea, as Edward became a very wealthy man, owning, among many businesses, the Patapsco Iron Works at Gunpowder Falls. Edward married Sidney Smith, the daughter of Revolutionary War hero General Samuel Smith. William Patterson apparently considered Edward highly responsible, for he charged Edward with the care of his sister, Betsy Patterson Bonaparte, and in his will left Edward the property upon which the family burial ground is located.

Accompanying Marianne Caton, the widow of his brother, to Paris in 1825, Edward Patterson very likely sat to West for this portrait during his stay there. His youthful appearance in West's painting, and West's known involvement with the Caton sisters in Paris, make this a more probable occasion for the sitting than during West's later Baltimore phase, when Patterson would have been at least forty-eight.

That West maintained his connection with the Pattersons is well known. During his Baltimore phase, he copied Gilbert Stuart's portraits of General and Mrs. Samuel Smith, Mrs. Patterson's parents.

21.

Edward John Trelawny

1792–1881

Oil on canvas, 69.8 x 55.3 cm. (27½ x 21¾ in.)
1829
Source of attribution: family documentation
Private collection

Not in exhibition

Edward John Trelawny was the younger son of a prominent Cornish family. Harshly treated by his father, he left home at age thirteen, joined the British Navy, sailed to India, and deserted in Bombay. He then became a pirate on the Indian Ocean. His *Adventures of a Younger Son* (1831), recording these experiences, enjoyed a wide audience in the nineteenth century.

Between 1820 and 1823, Trelawny was intimately involved with the Byron and Shelley entourage. After the capsize of the *Don Juan* on July 8, 1822, it was he who recovered Shelley's body. His *Recollections of Byron and Shelley* (1858) records Shelley's cremation, during which the author claims to have retrieved Shelley's heart which, he also claims, had survived the flames intact. He ordered a tomb for it in the Protestant Cemetery in Rome, in which he would himself be buried in 1881. In Trelawny's account of that fateful summer—at the time West was painting Byron's portrait—he never mentions West.

It has long been thought that West painted Trelawny at the time of the Byron encounter. It seems far more likely, in the absence of a reported introduction, that West painted this portrait during Trelawny's visit to England in 1828. The likeness was exhibited at the Royal Academy the following year.

The very model of the Byronic hero, Trelawny was tall, "powerfully built," according to his contemporaries, and surprisingly dark for an Englishman. West's depiction of his physicality has a strength, dash, and bravura that places it among the painter's very best works.

22.

Louis McLane

1786–1857

Oil on canvas, 96.5 x 77.5 cm. (38 x 30½ in.)
1829
Author's attribution, based on materials in William
Edward West's Papers, Archives of American Art, and
in the J. Hall Pleasants Files, Maryland Historical Society
University of Delaware, Newark, Delaware

Louis McLane was born in Smyrna, Delaware. Admitted to the bar in 1807, he opened his practice in Smyrna, and there, in 1812, married Catherine Mary Milligan. He was elected to the House of Representatives in 1817, and ten years later entered the Senate. In 1829 Andrew Jackson appointed him minister to Great Britain, charging him with improving trade between the two countries, and it was at this time, while he was in London, that William Edward West painted his portrait.

McLane had a long career in numerous public service roles—among them Jackson's Secretary of the Treasury, president of the Morris Canal and Banking Company in New York City, and participant in the Maryland Constitutional Convention of 1850. On his way to take up the presidency of the Baltimore and Ohio Railroad in 1837, he journeyed with West from New York to Baltimore. McLane's great goal was to be appointed to the Supreme Court, but this was never realized. "Jackson doubtless rendered him a service by not elevating him to the bench," the *Dictionary of American Biography* observes, "for his temperament was far from being judicial."

23.

Joshua Bates

1788–1864

Oil on canvas, 113.7 x 90.2 cm. (44¾ x 35½ in.)

Circa 1830–1835

Source of attribution: materials in the Frick Art Reference Library and the J. Hall Pleasants Files, Maryland Historical Society

Trustees of the Boston Public Library, Boston, Massachusetts

Joshua Bates was born in Weymouth, Massachusetts, to Colonel Joshua and Tirzah Pratt Bates. After a business failure following the War of 1812, he was sent to England by the shipping magnate William Grey, and achieved great success as an agent for American business interests abroad. In 1826 he joined with John Baring, a son of Sir Thomas Baring of the Baring investment group. They formed the financial house Baring Brothers and Company, in which Bates became senior partner and major stockholder.

As a member of the American community in London, Bates was acquainted with West. West painted a cabinet portrait of the young Bates son, who was subsequently killed in a shooting accident. We know that West was frequently at the Bates's country house, for several of Felicia Hemans's letters were sent there. When West's financial difficulties began in 1836, Joshua Bates lent him money, which he carefully repaid; Bates declined any interest on the loan.

Joshua Bates's great philanthropic interest was in the Public Library of Boston, to which he donated fifty thousand dollars, and an equal amount in books. In gratitude, the Library designated him a Founder, and named the main reading area Bates Hall.

This, West's only extant three-quarter-length portrait, is his largest and most ambitious. It was engraved in his day by J. Cheney.

24.

"Annette Delarbre"

Oil on canvas, 112.7 x 142.5 cm. (44⅜ x 56⅛ in.)
1831
Munson-Williams-Proctor Institute, Utica, New York

Washington Irving's writings provided two subjects for his "friend, West, the painter"—the painting based on *Pride of the Village* and this one, illustrating a story from *Bracebridge Hall* (1822).

Irving's heroine, Annette Delarbre, is the daughter of a Normandy farmer; Eugène Leforque, a neighbor boy, has been her sweetheart from childhood. The story recounts a disastrous series of lovers' misunderstandings which keep them apart; West's picture shows Annette in the depth of depression, numbed and stunned after learning that her lover has been lost at sea. She stands in the center of the picture, surrounded by her friends and family. Her father is holding her hand and beseeching her to return to her senses. Her left arm is held by Eugène's mother, a widow. A friend immediately behind the bereft maiden points to her own brow with a look of suggested dementia, while all the others gaze on Annette in grave concern.

Annette vows that Eugène will return when "the trees put on their blossoms and the swallow comes back over the sea." Eugène does survive his misadventure, and Irving's story ends happily with their marriage.

West's painting was exhibited at the Royal Academy in 1831 as *A Domestic Affliction,* and it was the picture West claimed got him the greatest attention in England. It is certainly one of his finest non-portrait works, beautifully colored and well composed. It makes great use of the forest as a backdrop, as well as an atmospheric chapel in the top right corner. As in *The Present* [Cat. no. 25], the figures themselves are rather flat, almost a frieze of faces across the picture plane. West's mannerist infatuation appears in the modeling of the father's hands and the awkward pose of the lady on the right with her back to the viewer.

25.

"The Present"

Oil on canvas, 96.5 x 80 cm. (38 x 31½ in.)
1833
Signed on the central figure's belt: "WEWestpinxit"
The J. B. Speed Art Museum, Louisville, Kentucky

West painted several pictures utilizing bridal themes: *The Unwilling Bride* and *Adornment of the Bride* are frequently mentioned in his papers. In *The Present,* a young bride-to-be is examining a gift of jewelry in the company of a group of women who are perhaps family and friends, and who seem to have mixed emotions about her good fortune.

West first exhibited this genre painting at the British Institution in 1833. Whether he left it behind in England when he returned to America in 1837, or reclaimed it at a later date, is uncertain. It was exhibited at the American Art Union in May of 1849, and was purchased by James M. Russell, at which time the variety of facial expressions in it was remarked upon very favorably. *The American Art Union Bulletin* (May 1849) observed a "contrast of expression in this picture; curiosity, carelessness, envy." Indeed, the facial expressions form a kind of frieze across the center of the picture plane, creating a compendium of human emotions. The composition is reminiscent of *The Muses* in its self-conscious, mannerist attempt at intricate arrangements heightening perspective and depth.

26.

Ellen Ward Gilmor

1811–1880

Oil on canvas, 76.2 x 63.5 cm. (30 x 25 in.)
Circa 1837–1841
The Maryland Historical Society, Baltimore, Maryland,
Gift of Mrs. Thomas G. Buchanan, Sr.

Ellen Ward was the daughter of a Baltimore judge, and married Robert Gilmor III in 1832. Robert Gilmor III was the nephew of the legendary Robert Gilmor of Baltimore, the first serious art collector in America. Ellen lived with her husband in a gothic-revival castle, named Glen Ellen for her, inspired by the writings of Sir Walter Scott and designed by the architect A. J. Davis. Mr. Gilmor's reach may have exceeded his grasp, for the castle was never completed beyond the second floor. Even in an unfinished state, the house contained twenty-five bedrooms.

According to a contemporary account, Mrs. Gilmor was "cherished as one of the most admired ladies that ever graced Baltimore society. Besides great beauty she was rarely endowed, with engaging manners and a disposition so good, so gentle and so sweet as to win friends on every side and amongst all classes." Six of her sons fought for the Confederacy during the War Between the States; two of them were killed, while a third, Harvey, became a famous cavalry leader.

This portrait is an example of West's Baltimore formula at its very best, especially the serenely beautiful eyes, much admired by the nineteenth-century art critic John Neal: "The eyes of West were wonders—irridescent, clear, and changeable."

27.

Ann McKim Handy

1802–1883

Oil on canvas, 76.2 x 63.5 cm. (30 x 25 in.)

Circa 1837–1841

The Maryland Historical Society, Baltimore, Maryland,
Gift of Dr. Lawrence R. Wharton, Jr., in memory of his
mother, Mrs. Lawrence R. Wharton, Sr.

Ann McKim Handy was a member of the wealthy Quaker merchant family of
Baltimore, the McKims. They were staunch patriots during the Revolution and became
ardent abolitionists. A clipper ship named *Ann McKim* and launched by her father,
Isaac, was one of the fastest of its type. West's portrait of her, with stylish corkscrew
curls and a rather prominent bosom, would seem to take the subject rather far afield
from her Quaker roots. She married the Baltimore attorney Samuel J. K. Handy
in 1837, very near the time of the portrait.

28.

Reverdy Johnson

1796–1876

Oil on canvas, 91.5 x 71.8 cm. (36 x 28¼ in.)
Circa 1838–1841
The Maryland Historical Society, Baltimore, Maryland,
Gift of Mrs. Charles G. Kerr

Reverdy Johnson was born in Annapolis, Maryland, the son of Deborah Chieselen and John Johnson. He started his career as a lawyer in Upper Marlboro, Maryland, but soon began the practice in Baltimore which he pursued for more than sixty years. He was held in high regard for his professional excellence and superb memory. In the Dred Scott case, he represented the defense and won, sending Scott back to his servitude. An ardent Whig, he opposed the expansion of the United States into the Mexican territory. He sympathized with the South but opposed secession. He served in the United States Senate before the war and was Attorney-General under President Zachary Taylor. He was one of the organizers of the peace conference at the Willard Hotel that attempted to thwart the outbreak of hostilities between the Union and the Confederate States of America. Throughout the war, he was a voice of moderation. Reverdy Johnson was deeply opposed to the harsh policy of Reconstruction imposed upon the South by the Republican-controlled Congress. When the Senate attempted to indict Robert E. Lee on grounds of treason, Johnson was his most vocal supporter. He defended the Ku Klux Klan of South Carolina as well as Mrs. Mary Suratt, one of the accused in the Lincoln assassination conspiracy.

At the age of eighty, while dining with the Governor of Maryland in Annapolis, he mistook an open window for a door and, walking out, fell one floor to his death. No less than James Garfield, in a eulogy, observed, "I never looked upon his face without feeling that he was a Roman of the elder days, the very embodiment of rugged force and of that high culture which comes from continuous persistent work."

29.

John Hazelhurst Boneval Latrobe

1803–1891

Oil on canvas, 76.2 x 63.5 cm. (30 x 25 in.)
Circa 1837–1841
Author's attribution based on examination of material in
the J. Hall Pleasants Files, Maryland Historical Society
The Circuit Court for Baltimore City, Baltimore, Maryland

When John H. B. Latrobe was born, his father, Benjamin, was supervising architect of the United States Capitol (1803–1811). John was appointed a cadet at West Point, but left in his fourth year when his father died. Returning to Baltimore, he began a highly successful career as a railroad lawyer. He was counsel to the Baltimore and Ohio Railroad from its incorporation in 1827 until his death. He was also a talented artist, writer, and philanthropist. He founded the Maryland Institute of the Mechanic Arts in 1825, served as President of the American Colonization Society, and prepared the first map of Liberia. He once sponsored a literary competition which awarded a prize to Edgar Allan Poe. When his second wife, Charlotte Virginia Claiborne of Mississippi, complained of the cold, he invented the Latrobe stove.

An accomplished watercolorist, he copied this portrait by West for several of his children, including his son Ferdinand, who was seven times mayor of Baltimore. Mrs. Latrobe was also painted by West, and her Mississippi background may have provided West's introduction to them.

105

30

Mary Ann Randolph Custis Lee

1808–1873

Oil on canvas, 76.2 x 63.5 cm. (30 x 25 in.)

March 1838

Washington-Custis-Lee Collection, Washington and Lee
University, Lexington, Virginia

Mary Lee's frantic letter home to her mother, in March 1838, asking for "Robert's uniform coat & epaulettes which are in that wooden box of papers," reveals that Robert E. Lee wanted to have West paint her portrait, "but I think I would prefer Sully."

Mary Lee had a mind of her own. She taught the slaves at Arlington to read and write, despite the laws of Virginia, and she always showed a greater interest in her cultural pursuits than in housekeeping. She supported neither slavery nor secession, and at the beginning of the war was an ardent Unionist. Throughout the war, she lived in a rented house in Richmond, and organized knitting sessions and wrapped countless bandages. Increasingly the victim of arthritis, she had become a semi-invalid by the time her husband and three sons returned from the war. The loss of Arlington House and its contents was a bitter blow from which she never recovered.

31.

Robert Edward Lee

1807–1870

Oil on canvas, 76.2 x 63.5 cm. (30 x 25 in.)

March 1838

Washington-Custis-Lee Collection, Washington and Lee
University, Lexington, Virginia

During the winter of 1837–1838, General Lee was on leave at Arlington, his wife's ancestral seat across the Potomac River from the capital city, waiting for Congress to allocate funds to complete an engineering project in St. Louis. It was a plan, being executed by him and Montgomery C. Meigs, to divert the Mississippi River from making a sandbar in front of the St. Louis harbor at the time when that city was the scene of most westward trade, and a takeoff point for the pioneers. By March, Congress had allocated sixty-five thousand dollars, and the Lees set off for St. Louis by way of Baltimore and Pittsburgh.

Mrs. Lee persuaded her husband to sit to William Edward West in Baltimore. As Mrs. Lee felt he should be depicted in full dress uniform, wearing his epaulettes, an urgent request was sent back to his mother-in-law, Mrs. Custis, to send his full regalia "up on the cars" to Baltimore. Mary Lee, Robert wrote in an addendum to her letter, "appeared so anxious to have my portrait taken that I could not decline gratifying her." The result is the first life-portrait of Lee, the "handsomest man in the army" and "the model of a soldier and the beau-ideal of a Christian man," according to Meigs. Posterity is more familiar with the somber gray-clad Lee, exhausted and defeated by a devastating war, but noble and revered, seated upon his charger, Traveller.

At an interesting juncture in both their lives, West has captured the young and vital Lee in a portrait which may have greater significance than the Byron likeness, the source of West's fame during his lifetime. The Lees themselves must have cherished this portrait, for it was among the few possessions Mrs. Lee took with her to the rented house in Richmond where she would sit out the war. The rest of their belongings were seized by Federal forces, along with Arlington House.

A photograph of the interior of the President's home at Washington and Lee University shows the portrait hanging over the mantel in the parlor, and today it hangs in the Lee Chapel there, near his office and below the marble effigy galvanizing him forever as an old man, worn out by a futile endeavor, yet triumphant in his last efforts as an educator and shining exemplar of profound integrity.

32.

Susan Haslett McKim

1780–1876

Oil on canvas, 76.2 x 63.5 cm. (30 x 25 in.)
Circa 1837–1841
The Maryland Historical Society, Baltimore, Maryland,
Gift of Mrs. Andrew Robeson

Susan Haslett was born in Caroline County, Maryland, and married William Duncan McKim, of the Baltimore merchant family, in 1806. They had six children, one of whom, Haslett, lived in London after 1834 and tended their business there. He would almost certainly have known the rest of the Baltimore merchant mafia then in London and surrounding the various Patterson-Caton connections. This would have given West ample introduction and currency for the portrait.

33.

Annie Campbell Gordon Thomas

1819–1886

Oil on canvas, 76.2 x 63.5 cm. (30 x 25 in.)
Circa 1838
The Baltimore Museum of Art, Baltimore, Maryland

Mrs. Thomas was the daughter of Basil Gordon, a wealthy Virginia merchant. She married John Hanson Thomas on November 15, 1837, when barely eighteen, and the portraits of herself and her husband may be a wedding pair. She and Dr. Thomas were the parents of seven children, and these pictures became separated by lateral descent.

The likeness of Mrs. Thomas is richly colored, and utilizes a vase of flowers on the subject's left very like those in *The Muses.*

34.

John Hanson Thomas

1813–1881

Oil on canvas, 76.2 x 63.5 cm. (30 x 25 in.)

Circa 1838

The Maryland Historical Society, Baltimore, Maryland,
Gift of Mrs. Edward Oppersdorf

John Hanson Thomas was resident physician of the Baltimore Infirmary. He surely prospered in that capacity, for at the time of his death he was president of the Farmers and Merchant Bank.

He is depicted here looking completely away from the artist, a convention West rarely used. It is interesting to compare this portrait by West, and the companion piece of his wife, to the portraits of the Lees done in the same period. In both pairs, the male figure dominates the picture plane, while the female figure is seen in more diminutive, albeit detailed, terms. Hung side by side, West's *Dr. Thomas* seems to stare onto his wife as a true pendant, while she, the young bride, looks meekly out at the viewer.

The two portraits belong to different institutions in the same community.

35.

Margaret Patterson Turner

1816–1873

Oil on canvas, 76.2 x 63.5 cm. (30 x 25 in.)
Circa 1838
The Maryland Historical Society, Baltimore, Maryland,
Gift of Mrs. Andrew Robeson

Margaret Patterson Turner was the daughter of the Baltimore merchant and West subject, Edward Patterson, and the wife of Charles Cocke Turner. Here West uses several conventions that he had developed while abroad, and which are also evident in his paintings *The Muses* and *The Present*. The strand of hair, just separating from the mass and beginning to droop forward, the distant moody landscape glimpsed through the opening on the left, and the rather trussed-up bodice are all typical of this period of his work.

36.

William Hickling Prescott

1796–1859

Oil on canvas, 74.9 x 62.2 cm. (29½ x 24½ in.)

Circa 1844

Source of attribution: portrait extant in the West estate, and presented to the Tennessee Historical Society by Mrs. John Trimble in 1860

Tennessee State Museum, Tennessee Historical Society Collection, Nashville, Tennessee

William Hickling Prescott was born into a prominent Boston family, and attended Harvard College. In his junior year he was hit in the left eye with a hard crust of bread, and immediately lost all vision in that eye. Two years later the surviving right eye became subject to severe inflammation, and, for all practical purposes, Prescott was blind. It is therefore all the more remarkable that he became the most famous historian in the antebellum period. His writings focused upon various aspects of Spanish colonial history, notably the reigns of Ferdinand and Isabella, Phillip II, and Charles V. It is for his multivolume histories of the conquests of Mexico and Peru that he was best known in his own time.

West was surely introduced to Prescott by Washington Irving, with whom Prescott had been corresponding since 1839. The exchange between the two men led to Irving's withdrawal from his own project, to write about the conquest of Mexico, in favor of Prescott. That volume appeared in 1843, and the Peruvian volume four years later. It seems likely that West painted Prescott's portrait while he was recuperating between the two volumes and at the period of his greatest acquaintance with the Irving circle. The portrait was never completed, and it remained in West's possession until his death. A remark made by Prescott while writing a biographical sketch of Sir Walter Scott, his great hero, is a helpful reminder: *It is, indeed, difficult to prescribe any precise rule by which the biographer should be guided in exhibiting the peculiarities, and still more the defects, of his subject. He should, doubtless, be slow to draw from obscurity those matters which are of a strictly personal and private nature, particularly when they have no material bearing on the character of the individual. But whatever the latter has done, said, or written to others, can rarely be made to come within this rule.*

37.

Warren Delano

1809–1899

Oil on canvas, 76.2 x 63.5 cm. (30 x 25 in.)
Circa 1845
Source of attribution: family documentation
The Houghteling Family

Warren Delano, one of two sons of Warren Delano, Senior, was a prosperous merchant in the China trade. He was the father of Sarah Delano, and thus Franklin Delano Roosevelt's grandfather. West became involved with the vast extended family of Delanos and Astors through Aaron Vail, and they proved to be the last of the large families to which he was attached. Among West's papers are several letters from Warren Delano and his wife, Dorah, as well as her sister, Laura Astor Delano.

After West had left New York, Warren Delano, in one of the last letters the artist kept, dated April 15, 1856, sent him best wishes. "I can assure you that you have left friends in New York who will have much pleasure in hearing from you—and the more so if they can hear of your continued good health—and your enjoyment of the scenes of your early life."

38.

Stephen Olin

1797–1851

Oil on canvas, 91.5 x 71.1 cm. (36 x 28 in.)
Circa 1845
Author's attribution
National Portrait Gallery, Smithsonian Institution,
Washington, D. C.

Stephen Olin was born in Leicester, Vermont, and attended Middlebury College, where it is thought that his rigorous studies ruined his health for life. In 1820 he moved to South Carolina, in search of a healthier climate, and there converted to Methodism and became a Methodist preacher. Although the itinerant existence was too strenuous for him, he remained a Methodist educator and lived in the South until 1837. Prior to becoming President of Randolph-Macon College in Virginia in 1834, he had been a professor of ethics and belles lettres at Franklin College, University of Georgia, Athens. From 1837 to 1840 he traveled abroad, largely in the Holy Land, to recover his health. His first wife, Mary Eliza Bostick of Milledgeville, Georgia, died in Naples while they were away. Olin returned to America and became President of Wesleyan University in 1842, a post he held until his death. He was actively involved in Methodist Church politics, especially the struggle to reach a stand on slavery. Olin had owned slaves while he lived in the South. One participant at the Methodist Conference of 1844 praised him as the only man in the church organization who understood both North and South. Throughout the 1840s he represented New York in Methodist conferences in the United States and in England.

Olin's tendency to ill health aged him greatly, and the portrait by West, painted in New York in the mid-1840s, seems to portray a much older man. This painting was once folded under to achieve a smaller size, and has suffered in restretching. The surface has been rather severely abraded. None of the damage, however, obscures the strong focus achieved by the proximity of the figure to the picture plane, nor the combination of compassion and shrewdness in the eyes, always West's best feature.

39.

Ann Sands Tucker Beck

1812–1903

Oil on canvas, 76.2 x 63.5 cm. (30 x 25 in.)
Circa 1840–1850
Unlocated

Photographs of the Beck and Jones portraits, which remain unlocated, are appropriate in a catalogue of West's work for what they tell us of the post-Baltimore phase of his career. While in Baltimore, fresh from his years abroad in Europe and anxious to recoup his losses, West employed a style closely related to the prevailing Romantic traits laid down by Sir Thomas Lawrence. After the move to New York, this formula—placing the figure close to the picture plane, emphasizing the bust and the neck line, and capturing the facial expression with as much characterization and emphasis upon the eyes as possible—begins to subtly expand. In both of these portraits, the modeling of the arms and the face allows a more sophisticated contouring to emerge. Both portraits have an expansive, almost languid sense of line, very reminiscent of the work of Jean-Auguste-Dominique Ingres, whom West would have encountered in France and England during his period abroad.

Unlike West's male subjects in this period, who appear sombre and older than their age, these women are presented at the height of elegance and fashion. During the 1840s and 1850s, West, having recovered his fortune in Baltimore, was again living among the wealthy and the socially prominent, this time in New York City. An entry in Washington Irving's journal for July 11, 1841, places West "Among the 4th of July guests at Mrs. Colford-Jones."

Both paintings attest to West's great abilities as a portraitist. In a period dominated by Sully, he transcends the flat, elliptical features favored by the popular taste, and paints in a more international style.

125

40.

Rebecca Mason Colford-Jones

lifedates unknown

Oil on canvas, 75.4 x 62.9 cm. (29¾ x 24¾ in.)
Circa 1841–1847
Unlocated

41.

"The Confessional"

Oil on canvas, 88.9 x 71.1 cm. (35 x 28 in.)
Circa 1845–1850
The New-York Historical Society, New York City

The religious painting *The Confessional* belongs to the brief period of the Gothic Revival in America, just beginning as West returned from Europe. Not only does the picture utilize such gothic elements as tracery and stained glass, but it is gothic in mood and theme as well. A young woman at her prayers confesses to an elderly priest as a soft, glowing light enters from the window at the right, an effect which the critic Richard Grant White found "brilliant and judiciously managed."

The Confessional was bought by the collector Thomas Jefferson Bryan, and was included in the catalogue of Bryan's collection, *Christian Art,* written by White in 1853. White's only biographical observation about the artist is, "Mr. West is a well known painter living in New York." The Bryan collection was given to the New-York Historical Society in 1867. Tuckerman recalls that the painting was a particular favorite of Irving's.

42.

Abigail Brown Brooks Adams

1808–1889

Oil on canvas, 75.6 x 62.2 cm. (29¾ x 24½ in.)
1847

Adams National Historic Site, Quincy, Massachusetts

Not in exhibition

Abigail Brown Brooks Adams was one of seven children of Peter Chardon
Brooks, and shared in his two-million-dollar estate, a fact noted rather blandly in her
son's autobiography, *The Education of Henry Adams.* In 1829 she married Charles
Francis Adams, son and grandson of United States Presidents, and himself a respected
diplomat and politician. She seems to have been a rather lively and enjoyable person,
free from the Adams gloom. She accompanied her husband to England in 1861 when
he began his stint as minister to the Court of St. James's, where "her success and
popularity . . . exceeded that of her husband," according to her son. Henry Adams's
only other remark about his mother claims that she "averred that every woman who
lived in a certain time in England came to look and dress like an Englishwoman,
no matter how she struggled."

Abigail Adams does not look especially English in West's portrait of her; indeed
she looks rather Southern, which may have appalled the Anglophobic, radical aboli-
tionist Adams even more. Her hair is painted in West's classic Baltimore manner, one
strand just separated and falling from the mass. An ample bosom, sweeping neckline,
and brilliantly colored attire complete the effect. West painted Mrs. Adams in
August of 1847, under instruction from her father. He was paid the sum of $175
for the work.

An invitation to dine with the Adams family is among the notes in the West
Papers. Unfortunately, Henry Adams, either absent or unconscious of the moment,
leaves us no impression of the painter of Byron and Lee.

43.

Edward Turner

1778–1860

Oil on canvas, 74.9 x 61.6 cm. (29½ x 34¼ in.)
Circa 1848–1850
Source of attribution: Colonial Dames,
Louisiana Portraits, p. 251
Mrs. Gaillard Conner and Mrs. Mary C. Stern

Edward Turner shared a similar ancestry and early development with William Edward West. He was born in Fairfax County, Virginia, in 1778, but was brought by his family to Kentucky in 1786, two years before West was born and about the time West's father was setting up shop in High Street. Turner was educated at Transylvania College in Lexington, and was admitted to the bar in Kentucky. By 1802 he had moved to Natchez, Mississippi, following the pattern of Jefferson Davis's family. He served in the territorial legislature of Mississippi, and was a private secretary to Governor Claiborne. Immediately before Mississippi attained statehood in 1817, he compiled a digest of the territorial statutes which formed the basis for the Mississippi State Code. From 1817 to 1848, he served in various capacities in the state government, including nine years as the Judge of the High Court of Errors and Appeals. When he retired from the bench in 1844, he entered the State Senate, and remained there for four years. At the age of seventy, he left public life, and lived quietly at his plantation, Woodlands, near Natchez.

Judge Turner invited West to spend the winter of 1857, the last of West's life, at Woodlands. "We can make you very comfortable," he writes on August 24, 1856, "and give you full employment for your pencil." Lest West fear that Natchez had not transcended its frontier phase, he adds reassuring lines concerning many of West's old friends—the Davis, Quitman, Bingaman, Chotard, and Evans families. Turner writes that all have "beautiful and highly improved seats." Nor will West be culturally isolated, as "most have large libraries and take many of the European and American periodicals." Evidence of West's affability and enduring popularity, in both North and South, is presented in Judge Turner's closing remarks. "We all want to see you . . . write me soon . . . you know how much I will appreciate a good long letter from you."

Edward Turner is mentioned in some accounts as having befriended West during his stay in Natchez in 1818–1819. It seems likely that this portrait was painted in New York during a vacation back East which Judge Turner took with his wife, Eliza Baker, after his retirement. A Victorian account of his life, published in the *Memoirs of Mississippi* in 1891, recalled that the Judge was "esteemed for his rare conversational powers, his gracious and deferential manners."

133

44.

Eliza Baker Turner

1789–1878

Oil on canvas, 74.9 x 61.6 cm. ((29½ x 24¼ in.)

Circa 1848–1850

Author's attribution based on material in William Edward
West Papers, Archives of American Art, Smithsonian
Institution, and in Colonial Dames, *Louisiana Portraits*, p. 251

Mrs. Gaillard Conner and Mrs. Mary C. Stern

Eliza Baker was a native of New Jersey, and married Edward Turner in 1812. They had four children, two of whom died in infancy, and she was survived by two daughters, Mary Louisa Turner McMurran and Elizabeth Frances Turner Conner. She outlived her husband by eighteen years and, unlike him, saw war and Reconstruction come to Mississippi, along with a decline in her personal fortunes. Her daughter, Mary Louisa, returned to live with her after the loss of her own home, Melrose, during the Reconstruction, and after the death of her husband in a steamboat disaster. At the time of Mrs. Turner's death, her home, Woodlands Plantation, had declined to seventy-five acres, and the large fortune in land and investments which Judge Turner had accumulated was substantially diminished.

45.

Elizabeth Henrietta Young and *Anna Elizabeth Mercer*

1797–1870   1832–1851

Oil on canvas, 124.4 x 99 cm. (49 x 39 in.)
Circa 1852
Note on back of canvas: "return to Mr. West"
William Barrow Floyd

Correspondence from Elizabeth Young in the West Papers indicates that this portrait was commissioned for her niece, Jane Metcalfe, whose daughter was named Ann Mercer Metcalfe. Miss Young was the sister of Benjamin F. Young of Natchez, whom West also painted. Miss Mercer was the daughter of Dr. William Newton Mercer of Natchez and New Orleans.

The commission called for a portrait "taken of my child and self grouped in some simple and natural manner." Miss Young writes in her letter that West's suggestion along the lines of his *Pride of the Village* "would be too painful." Elizabeth Young had been a companion to Miss Mercer, recently dead of tuberculosis. The niece for whom the portrait was intended "would like the picture more as she used to see us— sitting together—my child perhaps with a book in her hand from which she had just read some passage—."

West seems to have had some personal contact with Miss Young, in order to paint her portrait, but the likeness of Miss Mercer was taken from a daguerreotype. All of this may account for the strong contrast of facial expressions in the picture— Miss Young seen in a realistic light, clad in black mourning, and Miss Mercer looking off into the distance, dressed all in white and somewhat unfocused. It is a unique West painting, combining elements of his genre and literary work with portraiture.

Miss Young's last letter to him indicates that she was traveling north and was "very anxious to see the *picture,* but I beg you to allow me to do so when no one— not even yourself should be present." Such was the extent of the grief which prompted this amazing memorial.

137

46.

Laura Sevier Norvell

1825–1895

Oil on canvas, 76.2 x 63.5 cm. (30 x 25 in.)
Circa 1856
Source of attribution: family documentation
Gertrude McNabb Meissner

Laura Jane Sevier married West's nephew, Henry Lawrence Norvell, in Nashville in 1842. His mother, West's younger sister, Hannahretta West Norvell, had lived in Nashville since her marriage in 1814 to Moses Norvell. Several of West's brothers and sisters, including John B., Sarah, and Hannahretta, lived in Nashville, and it was there that he returned at the end of his life. Mrs. Dunn's article and written accounts by West's niece, Aduella Norvell, recall how his last years in Nashville were kept quite busy painting portraits of various nieces and nephews. This portrait is a fine example of West's late style. A great deal of attention has been paid to coloration and background detail. It has descended in the same branch of his family that also owned his remaining letters and manuscripts.

NOTES ON SOURCES

CATALOGUE NUMBER 1. Samuel McCullough's recollection of Edward West, Jr., as a man "of all work, all ideas . . ." is from Marion Mulligan Ross, "Story of West, Painter . . .," *Lexington* (Kentucky) *Leader,* May 1, 1921, Sunday supplement (unpaged).

CATALOGUE NUMBER 4. Critic E. L. Tinker's appraisal of Poydras's poem is cited from the entry for Poydras in the *Dictionary of American Biography,* vol. 15 (New York, 1935), p. 164.

CATALOGUE NUMBER 7. Jefferson Davis's letter (posted from Beauvoir, Mississippi) in which he attributes the portrait of his father to West is published in the *Davis Family Association News letter* for March 1980.

CATALOGUE NUMBERS 8 AND 9. The Dunbars' management of their farm and household was commented upon by Solon Robinson, "A Mississippi Plantation," *The Cultivator* 3 (1846) : 31

CATALOGUE NUMBER 10. The contemporary description of John Richards was found in the curatorial files (under his name) in the Old Capitol Museum, Jackson, Mississippi.

CATALOGUE NUMBER 14. The most thorough account of the provenance of this portrait is found in John Clubbe's article "William Edward West's Portrait of Teresa Guiccioli," *Byron Journal* (1979) : 76–87.

CATALOGUE NUMBER 18. Washington Irving's note that Dominick Lynch, Jr., sat to West is in William P. Trent and George S. Hellman, eds., *The Journals of Washington Irving,* vol. 2 (Boston, 1919), pp. 75–76, 89.

CATALOGUE NUMBER 19. Washington Irving's recollection that the Caton sisters sat to West is in Washington Irving, *Journals and Notebooks,* ed. Walter Reichert, vol. 3 (Madison, Wis., 1970), pp. 439 and 443.

CATALOGUE NUMBER 26. The contemporary account of Mrs. Gilmor's virtues was found in the Gilmor family files, Maryland Historical Society, Baltimore; John Neal's comment on the "eyes of West" is from *Selections from the Writings of John Neal* (State College, Pa., 1943), p. 81.

CATALOGUE NUMBER 30. The sitter's letter to her mother, Mrs. George Washington Parke Custis, is dated March 24, 1838, from Baltimore, and is in the archives of the Virginia Historical Society, Richmond.

CATALOGUE NUMBER 36. Prescott's remarks about the biographer's art are from *Essays of American Essayists* (New York, 1900), p. 104.

CATALOGUE NUMBER 37. Warren Delano's letter to West is in the William Edward West Papers, Archives of American Art, Smithsonian Institution.

CATALOGUE NUMBER 41. Richard Grant White's appraisal of *The Confessional,* and his very brief note about West, were published in *A Companion to the Thomas J. Bryan Gallery of Christian Art* (New York, 1853), which is on microfilm (roll P38, frames 657–736) in the Archives of American Art, Smithsonian Institution.

CATALOGUE NUMBER 42. Henry Adams's recollections about his mother are in his autobiography, *The Education of Henry Adams* (Cambridge, Mass., 1918)—her inherited wealth on page 23 and both her popularity in England and her comment on Englishwomen's looks and dress on page 211.

CATALOGUE NUMBER 43. Judge Turner's letter of invitation to West, dated August 24, 1856, from Woodlands (near Natchez, Mississippi), is in the William Edward West Papers, Archives of American Art, Smithsonian Institution; the recollections about Judge Turner are in Goodspeed & Co., *Memoirs of Mississippi* (Chicago, 1891), p. 929.

CATALOGUE NUMBER 45. Miss Young's letter to West, commissioning the portrait "of my child and self," is dated November 2, 1852, from the St Nicholas Hotel in Cincinnati, and is in the William Edward West Papers, Archives of American Art, Smithsonian Institution.

Checklist WITH NOTES

In this checklist I have made an entry for each work by West for which I found a reference: in lists of exhibitions, in the literature, in public collections, or in various scholarly centers. All attributions that I consider unlikely or questionable are nevertheless included as part of the literature. I have not included any reference to portraits of the Astor family mentioned in the family correspondence, for nowhere else—including mention in the extensive correspondence between Margaret Astor and West—do I encounter the existence of actual objects.

ABBREVIATIONS FOR REFERENCES

ANDREWS:
A list of family portraits compiled by Mrs. Forrest Andrews in 1962 as part of her research on the West family. Mrs. Andrews's husband was a descendant of John B. West. The list is in the West Papers at the Archives of American Art, Smithsonian Institution, Washington, D. C.

CAP:
Catalog of American Portraits, National Portrait Gallery, Smithsonian Institution, Washington, D. C.

FARL:
Frick Art Reference Library, New York City.

IAP:
Inventory of American Painting, National Museum of American Art, Smithsonian Institution, Washington, D. C.

JHP:
J. Hall Pleasants Files, Maryland Historical Society, Baltimore.

TSL:
Tennessee State Library, Nashville.

WITT:
Witt Art Reference Library, The Courtauld Institute, London, England.

WHITLEY:
Edna Talbott Whitley, *Kentucky Ante-Bellum Portraiture* (Richmond, Va., 1956).

ABIGAIL BROWN BROOKS (Mrs. Charles Francis) ADAMS (1808–1889), oil on canvas, 75.6 x 62.2 cm. (29¾ x 24½ in.), 1847. Adams National Historic Site, Quincy, Massachusetts. *Illustrated on page 131.*

ADORNMENT OF THE BRIDE, oil on canvas, 91.9 x 74.9 cm. (36 x 28½ in.). Unlocated.

Last exhibited in "Tennessee Painting—The Past," Cheekwood, Nashville, Tennessee, 1960. West exhibited no painting by this title in his life, but it was reproduced in a newspaper article on him published in the *Nashville Banner*, April 7, 1929. It was then listed as the property of a West descendant.

ALLEGRO, A STUDY. Unlocated.

Exhibited at the British Institution, 1829.

CECILIA ANNE WINDHAM (Mrs. Henry) BARING, circa 1830–37. Unlocated.

FARL, Witt.

HENRY BARING, ESQ., WITH GAMEKEEPERS. Unlocated.

Exhibited at the Royal Academy in 1832.

CAPTAIN JOSHUA BARNEY (1759–1818), oil on canvas, 68.5 x 55.8 cm. (27 x 22 in.). Private collection.

Unlikely attribution. FARL, CAP.

HARRIET COLE (MRS. JOSHUA) BARNEY (died 1849), oil on canvas. Unlocated.

Unlikely attribution. FARL.

JOSHUA BATES (1788–1864), oil on canvas, 113.6 x 90.2 cm. (44¾ x 35½ in.), circa 1830–35, Trustees' Room, Boston Public Library. *Illustrated on page 93.*

Engraved by Cheney. FARL, CAP.

THE BATHING GIRL. Unlocated.

Mentioned in newspaper clipping as having been sold at West's death. TSL.

THE BATTLE OF NEW ORLEANS, circa 1815. Unlocated. *Illustrated on page 5.*

Mentioned in *The Album of American Battle Art, 1755–1918* (Washington, D. C., 1947). Engraved by Yeager.

MR. AND MRS. BEATTY, oil on canvas, 76.2 x 63.5 cm. (30 x 25 in.), circa 1837–40. Private collection.

Personal attribution based on close similarity to West's Baltimore phase. CAP.

ANN SANDS TUCKER (MRS. JOHN) BECK (1812–1903), oil on canvas, 76.2 x 63.5 cm. (30 x 25 in.), circa 1840–50. Unlocated. *IIlustrated on page 125.*

FARL.

CATHERINE SURGET BINGAMAN (1776–1841), oil on canvas, 91.5 x 71.1 cm. (36 x 28 in.), circa 1818. Linton Surget Collection, Tulane University Art Collection, New Orleans, Louisiana. *Illustrated on page 57.*

THEODORE BOLTON. Unlocated.

TSL.

JOSEPH BONAPARTE, The Court de Survilliers (1768–1844), 1833. Unlocated.

West painted Napoleon's brother on his visit, in 1833, to England from America, where he had taken refuge in Bordentown, New Jersey, following Waterloo. He sent the portrait to Joseph Hopkinson of Philadelphia, by way of an American diplomat. "I sent you by Mr. Hynes[?] of Baltimore, United States charge d'affaires in Sweden, who left here 10 days ago, my portrait painted in oil by Mr. West, an American artist, nephew of the famous West. I beg you to accept it as that of a friend" (Joseph Bonaparte to Joseph Hopkinson, August 24, 1833, letter no. 69, Hopkinson Papers, Historical Society of Pennsylvania). The two Josephs had been neighbors in Bordentown from 1820 to 1823.

West dined with Bonaparte in London in the company of Samuel Rogers on several occasions. Rogers referred to Bonaparte as "old Joe."

JOHN TUCKER BOWDOIN (1787–1821), oil on canvas, 76.2 x 63.5 cm. (30 x 25 in.), circa 1818. John Page Elliott. *Illustrated on page 59.*

CAP.

JAMES PERCY BROWN AND HIS SISTER SUSAN, oil on canvas, 58.4 x 74.9 cm. (23 x 29½ in.), circa 1818. Unlocated.

Sold at Sloan's auction house, Washington, D.C., February 28, 1933. These are the children of Dr. Samuel Brown and his wife, Catherine Percy. FARL.

DR. SAMUEL BROWN (1769–1830), oil on canvas, 83.8 x 71.1 cm. (33 x 28 in.), circa 1807, The University of Kentucky, Lexington. *Illustrated on page 51.*

FARL, CAP.

ADUELLA NORVELL (MRS. ALEXANDER) BRYANT (1849–1917), oil on canvas, 74.9 x 60.3 cm. (29½ x 23¾ in.), circa 1856. Unlocated.

Last exhibited in "Tennessee Painting—The Past," Cheekwood, Nashville, Tennessee, 1960. The subject was West's niece, who inherited several paintings. Family documents note that West was working on the portrait at the time of his death.

MRS. WILLIAMS BULKELEY. Unlocated.
Exhibited at the Royal Academy in 1829.

LADY ELIZABETH BURKE. Unlocated.
Exhibited at the Royal Academy in 1827.

GEORGE NOEL GORDON, 6th LORD BYRON (1788–1824), oil on canvas, 76.2 x 63.5 cm. (30 x 25 in.), 1822. National Portrait Gallery, Edinburgh, Scotland. *Illustrated on page 75.*

West copied the portrait frequently. Among extant versions are those at the John Hunt Morgan House in Lexington, Kentucky, and in the Washington University collection, St. Louis, Missouri.

GEORGE HENRY CALVERT (1803–1889), oil on canvas, 1839–41. Unlocated.

FARL, CAP.

COLONEL CHARLES CARROLL (1801–1862), oil on canvas, 91.5 x 71.1 cm. (36 x 28 in.), circa 1837–39. Private collection.

FARL, CAP.

CHARLES HENRY CARTER (1804–1872), oil on canvas, 76.2 x 63.5 cm. (30 x 25 in.), 1825. Private collection.

JHP.

CATON SISTERS AS THE THREE GRACES, oil on canvas, 55.8 x 68.5 cm. (22 x 27 in.), oval, circa 1828–32. Private collection.

The three Caton sisters were: Marianne Caton (1788–1853) (Mrs. Robert Patterson; Marchioness of Wellesley); Louisa Catherine Caton (1791–1874) (Lady Felton Elwell Bathurst-Hervey; Duchess of Leeds and Marchioness of Carmathen); Elizabeth Caton

(1794–1862) (Countess of Shrewsbury). The portrait is done as three floating heads and bears no compositional similarity to *The Muses.* JHP.

MRS. REBECCA MASON COLFORD-JONES, oil on canvas, 75.6 x 62.9 cm. (29¾ x 24¾ in.), 1841–47. Unlocated. *Illustrated on page 127.*
FARL.

THE CONFESSIONAL, oil on canvas, 88.9 x 71.1 cm. (35 x 28 in.), circa 1845–50. New-York Historical Society. *Illustrated on page 129.*
FARL.

WILLIAM CONNER, pastel on paper, 28.5 x 24.1 cm. (11¼ x 9½ in.), circa 1818. Shelburne Museum, Vermont.

Natchez subject, attribution unlikely. IAP.

COURTSHIP. Two paintings. Unlocated.

No additional information has come to light on the two paintings by this name that were exhibited at the British Institution in 1827, when West's address was given as 63 Margaret Street.

CUPID AND PSYCHE, oil on canvas. Unlocated. *Engraving illustrated on page 39.*

Almost certainly exhibited at the British Institution in 1826 as *Two Children with a Dove,* when West's address is given as 49 Leicester Square. Sold to American Art Union in 1849. Engraving of painting by William Humphreys in New York Public Library Print Collection.

JOSEPH EMERY DAVIS (1784–1870), oil on canvas, 68.6 x 55.9 cm. (27 x 22 in.), circa 1818. Percival T. Beacroft, Jr., Rosemont Plantation, Woodville, Mississippi. *Illustrated on page 61.*

WARREN DELANO (1809–1899), oil on canvas, 76.2 x 63.5 cm. (30 x 25 in.), circa 1845. The Houghteling Family. *Illustrated on page 121.*
FARL.

ANNETTE DELARBRE, oil on canvas, 112.7 x 142.5 cm. (44⅜ x 56⅛ in.), 1831. Munson-Williams-Proctor Institute, Utica, New York. *Illustrated on page 95.*

Engraved by Joseph Andrews. FARL.

JOSEPH DUNBAR (1783–1846), oil on canvas, 72.7 x 60 cm. (28⅝ x 23⅝ in.), circa 1818. Private collection. *Illustrated on page 63.*

Published in Sara Lewis Flanary, "William Edward West in New Orleans and Mississippi," *Antiques* 124, no. 5 (November 1983).

OLIVIA MAGRUDER DUNBAR (1786–1859), oil on canvas, 70.2 x 60 cm. (28⅝ x 23⅝ in.), circa 1818. Private collection. *Illustrated on page 65.*

Published in Sara Lewis Flanary, "William Edward West in New Orleans and Mississippi." *Antiques* 124, no. 5 (November 1983).

VALERIA WINCHESTER ERWIN (1835–1916). Unlocated.

Granddaughter of West's sister, Maria Creed West Price, whose daughter, Samuella Price, married Valerius Publicola Winchester in 1833. Andrews.

EMILY DOUGLAS SIMMS (MRS. FRENCH) FORREST (1810–1880), oil on canvas, 76.2 x 63.5 cm. (30 x 25 in.), 1837–40. Private collection. CAP.

FRENCH FORREST (1796–1866), oil on canvas, 76.2 x 63.5 cm. (30 x 25 in.), circa 1815–30. Private collection.

Unlikely attribution. *Mrs. Forrest,* however, is a typical Baltimore-phase portrait. CAP.

THOMAS R. FOSDICK (1797–1829), oil on panel, 66 x 53.3 cm. (26 x 21 in.), 1818. Cincinnati Historical Society, Cincinnati, Ohio. *Illustrated on page 71.*

Whitley.

MARY PAWLEY FRAZER. Unlocated.
PETER FRAZER. Unlocated.

Mrs. Frazer is unlikely to be a West; Mr. Frazer is typical of West's Baltimore phase. FARL.

THE FRISON GIRL. Unlocated.

Exhibited at the British Institution in 1834. A "Frison Girl" would hail from northern Holland.

ROBERT FULTON (1765–1815). Unlocated.

Engraving in National Portrait Gallery collection by Leney, engraved for the *Atlantic* magazine, circa 1815. CAP.

MRS. CHARLOTTE PATTERSON GILMOR (1821–1846), oil on canvas, 76.2 x 63.5 cm. (30 x 25 in.), circa 1839–41. Private collection. FARL, JHP.

ELLEN WARD (MRS. ROBERT) GILMOR (1803–1874), oil on canvas, 76.2 x 63.5 cm. (30 x 25 in.), circa 1837–41, Maryland Historical Society, Baltimore. *Illustrated on page 99.*

JHP, CAP, FARL (gives lifedates 1811–1880).

ELEANOR ADDISON SMITH (MRS. JOHN STERETT) GITTINGS (1799–1848), oil on canvas, 76.2 x 63.5 cm. (30 x 25 in.), circa 1840. Private collection.

JHP previously attributed this to O. T. Eddy.

MICHAEL GRATZ (1740–1811), pastel on paper, 61 x 50.8 cm. (24 x 20 in.), circa 1809. National Portrait Gallery, Smithsonian Institution. *Illustrated on page 53.*

REBECCA GRATZ (1781–1869), oil on canvas, circa 1809. Unlocated.

Reproduced in Nellie Porterfield Dunn, "An Artist of the Past: William Edward West and His Friends at Home and Abroad," *Putnam's Monthly,* September 1907. FARL, CAP.

TERESA GAMBA, COUNTESS GUICCIOLI (1803–1873), oil on canvas, 80 x 67.3 cm. (31½ x 26½ in.), 1822, Miami University Art Museum, Miami, Ohio. *Illustrated on page 77.*

TERESA GAMBA, COUNTESS GUICCIOLI (1803–1873), oil on canvas, 75 x 62.2 cm. (29½ x 24½ in.). Private collection.

Recently auctioned at California Book Auction Galleries, San Francisco, California (catalogue no. 313184, lot 69). The portrait could be by West, but is not of Teresa Guiccioli. The costume suggests the 1840–50 period. West and Guiccioli never met again after 1822.

ANN MCKIM (MRS. SAMUEL J. K.) HANDY (1802–1883), oil on canvas, 76.2 x 63.5 cm. (30 x 25 in.), circa 1837–41. Maryland Historical Society, Baltimore. *Illustrated on page 101.*

FARL, JHP, CAP.

CATHERINE HAYES (1825–1861), oil on canvas, 1851. Private collection.

Family documents in the West Papers suggest that the opera star was painted by West at the time of her first appearance in this country. The portrait has descended through West's family.

FELICIA HEMANS (1793–1835), oil on canvas, 1827. Unlocated. *Illustrated on page 26.*

An original and two copies were made, one for Charles Eliot Norton, and one which West kept.

LOUISA SOPHIA MEREDITH (MRS. GORDON GREEN) HOWLAND (1810–1888), oil on canvas, 76.2 x 63.5 cm. (30 x 25 in.), circa 1841–47. Private collection.
FARL.

LEIGH HUNT (1784–1859), oil on canvas, 22.8 x 18.4 cm. (9 x 7¼ in.), circa 1824. The University of Virginia Library, Charlottesville, Virginia. *Illustrated on page 81.*

WASHINGTON IRVING (1788–1859), oil on canvas. Unlocated.

Irving notes in his journal, April 3, 1825, "sit to West for sketch." Reproduced in Dunn, "Artist of the Past: West." CAP.

ISRAEL IN BABYLON. Unlocated.

Engraving in the New York Public Library print collection.

ITALIAN FLOWER GIRL. Unlocated.

Exhibited at the Royal Academy in 1826.

ANDREW JACKSON (1767–1854), oil on canvas, 91.4 x 68.5 cm (36 x 27 in.), circa 1855, after Samuel Lovett Waldo. Daughters of 1812, New Orleans, Louisiana.

AUGUST MCVICKAR (MRS. WILLIAM) JAY. Unlocated.
TSL.

REVERDY JOHNSON (1796–1876), oil on canvas, 91.4 x 71.8 cm. (36 x 28¼ in.), 1838–41. Maryland Historical Society, Baltimore. *Illustrated on page 103.*

JHP, FARL, CAP.

MRS. NANCY MOTLEY JONES, oil on canvas, 86.4 x 68.5 cm. (34 x 27 in.). Private collection.

Unlikely attribution. FARL.

MARY DEVEREUX COLT (MRS. AARON KEPPLE) JOSEPHS (1817–1854), oil on canvas, 76.2 x 63.5 cm. (30 x 25 in.), circa 1837–41. Private collection (Baltimore).
FARL.

JUDITH, oil on canvas, 132 x 104.1 cm. (52 x 41 in.). Unlocated. *Illustrated on page 35.*

Exhibited at the Royal Academy in 1833. Last known location: Tennessee State Museum, Nashville. FARL.

KATHERINE LIVINGSTON (MRS. WALTER) LANGDON, oil on canvas, 60.9 x 50.8 cm. (24 x 20 in.). Private collection.
FARL.

CHARLOTTE VIRGINIA CLAIBORNE (MRS. J. H. B.) LATROBE (1815–1903), oil on canvas, 74.9 x 63.2 cm. (29½ x 34½ in.), 1838–41. Unlocated.

At one point deposited in the Peale Museum, Baltimore. Attributed to Thomas Sully by Edward Biddle and Mantle Fielding, *The Life and Works of Thomas Sully (1783–1872)* (Philadelphia, 1921) as cat. no. 1029. Copied by J. H. B. Latrobe. FARL.

JOHN HAZELHURST BONEVAL LATROBE (1803–1891), oil on canvas, 76.2 x 63.5 cm. (30 x 25 in.), circa 1837–41. The Circuit Court for Baltimore City, Baltimore, Maryland. *Illustrated on page 105.*

Copied by J. H. B. Latrobe for his son. FARL, CAP.

W. B. LAWRENCE (Secretary of Legation of the Court of St. James's). Unlocated.

Exhibited at the Royal Academy, London, in 1827, and at the National Academy of Design in 1828.

MARY WEAVER (MRS. CHARLES LEONARD) LEBARON (1783–1865), oil on canvas, 76.2 x 63.5 cm. (30 x 25 in.), circa 1830?. Private collection.

Attribution and date by FARL are questionable. Reproduced in National Society of the Colonial Dames in the State of Alabama, *Alabama Portraits Prior to 1870* (Mobile, Ala., 1969), p. 209.

HENRY LEE (1756–1818), oil on canvas, 74.9 x 63.5 cm. (29 x 25 in.). Copy of Gilbert Stuart portrait. Private collection.

Attribution by Mrs. George Bolling Lee,

recorded in IAP, CAP. Previously on long-term loan to Virginia Historical Society.

MARY ANNE RANDOLPH CUSTIS (MRS. ROBERT EDWARD) LEE (1808–1873), oil on canvas, 76.2 x 63.5 cm. (30 x 25 in.), March 1838, Washington and Lee University, Lexington, Virginia. *Illustrated on page 107.*

CAP.

ROBERT EDWARD LEE (1807–1870), oil on canvas, 76.2 x 63.5 cm. (30 x 25 in.), March 1838, Washington and Lee University, Lexington, Virginia. *Illustrated on page 109, and on cover.*

CAP.

WILLIAM PRESSTMAN LEMMON (1794–1864), oil on canvas, 73.6 x 60.9 cm. (29 x 24 in.), circa 1837. Private collection.

Reproduced in National Society of Colonial Dames in the State of North Carolina, *North Carolina Portrait Index 1700–1860,* (Chapel Hill, 1963), p. 139.

LORD BYRON'S VISIT TO THE U. S. S. CONSTITUTION, May 21, 1822, oil on canvas, 30.4 x 40.6 cm. (12 x 16 in.), circa 1822–25. H. Richard Dietrich, Jr. *Illustrated on page 79.*

DOMINICK LYNCH, JR. (1786–1857), oil on canvas, 90.2 x 72.4 cm. (35½ x 28½ in.), 1824–25. New-York Historical Society. *Illustrated on page 83.*

DOMINICK LYNCH, JR. (1786–1857), oil on canvas, 76.2 x 63.5 cm. (30 x 25 in.), circa 1810–15. Long Island Historical Society, Brooklyn, New York.

Attribution unlikely. Previously dated 1825 based on Washington Irving's *Journals and Notebooks,* vol. 2 (Boston, 1819), pp. 75–76, 89.

COMMODORE ISAAC MAYO (1795–1861), oil on canvas, 76.2 x 63.5 cm. (30 x 25 in.), 1838. Private collection.

JHP.

SARAH BATTAILE FITZHUGH BLAND (MRS. ISAAC) MAYO (1807–1886), oil on canvas, 75.6 x 62.8 cm. (29¾ x 24¾ in.), circa 1838–41. Private collection.

FARL.

LYDIA MCCULLOUGH, miniature painted circa 1805–8. Unlocated.

Lost during War of 1812.

SUSAN HASLETT (MRS. WILLIAM DUNCAN) MCKIM (1780–1876), oil on canvas, 76.2 x 63.5 cm. (30 x 25 in.), circa 1837–41, Maryland Historical Society, Baltimore. *Illustrated on page 111.*

JHP.

LOUIS MCLANE (1786–1857), oil on canvas, 96.5 x 77.5 cm. (38 x 30½ in.), 1829. University of Delaware, Newark, Delaware. *Illustrated on page 91.*

LOUIS MCLANE II (1819–1905), oil on panel, 26 x 21.6 cm. (10¼ x 8½ in.), circa 1829–38. Private collection.

West frequently painted these small cabinet portraits of the sons of more famous sitters.

ROBERT MILLIGAN MCLANE (1815–1898), oil on panel, 26 x 21.6 cm. (10¼ x 8½ in.). Private collection.

Son of Louis McLane. FARL, JHP.

JOHN MINOR (1768–1832), oil on canvas, 73 x 60.3 cm. (28¾ x 23¾ in.), circa 1818. Private collection.

Reproduced in National Society of the Colonial Dames of America in the State of Louisiana, *Louisiana Portraits* (New Orleans, 1975), p. 187. Unlikely attribution.

THOMAS MOORE (1779–1852), oil on academy board, 27.9 x 22.8 cm. (11 x 9 in.), circa 1804. The Valentine Museum, Richmond, Virginia.

Attribution unlikely. Label attached in back states that the portrait was executed on Moore's visit to Richmond in 1804. West would have been only sixteen at that time, and this painting is more sophisticated than his early work.

THE MUSES OF PAINTING, POETRY, AND MUSIC, oil on canvas, 95.9 x 83.2 cm. (37¾ x 32¾ in.), circa 1825. Corcoran Gallery of Art, Washington, D. C. *Illustrated on page 85, and as frontispiece.*

LAURA SEVIER NORVELL (1825–1895), oil on canvas, 76.2 x 63.5 cm. (30 x 25 in.), circa 1856. Gertrude McNabb Meissner. *Illustrated on page 139.*

STEPHEN OLIN (1797–1851), oil on canvas, 91.5 x 71.1 cm. (36 x 28 in.), circa 1845. National Portrait Gallery, Smithsonian Institution, Washington, D.C. *Illustrated on page 123.*

EDWARD PATTERSON (1789–1865), oil on canvas, 76.2 x 63.5 cm. (30 x 25 in.), circa 1825. Maryland Historical Society, Baltimore. *Illustrated on page 87.*

FARL, JHP.

PORTRAIT OF ST. PETER. Unlocated.

Exhibited in 1817.

JULIEN DE LALLANDE POYDRAS (1740–1824), oil on canvas, 88.9 x 71.1 cm. (35 x 28 in.), circa 1817. The Poydras Home Board of Managers, New Orleans, Louisiana. *Illustrated on page 55.*

WILLIAM HICKLING PRESCOTT (1796–1859), oil on canvas, 74.9 x 62.2 cm. (29½ x 24½ in.), circa 1844 (unfinished). Tennessee State Museum, Nashville. *Illustrated on page 119.*

FARL.

THE PRESENT, oil on canvas, 96.5 x 80 cm. (38 x 31½ in.), 1833. J. B. Speed Art Museum, Louisville, Kentucky. *Illustrated on page 97.*

THE PRIDE OF THE VILLAGE. Unlocated.

This illustration of Washington Irving's story from *The Sketch Book* was first exhibited in London at the Royal Academy in 1830. It enjoyed a great popularity in engraved form. The original painting, along with *Annette Delarbre,* was part of Charles Eliot Norton's collection of West's paintings, and was last seen by Mrs. Dunn in Cambridge, Massachusetts. Of his heroine Irving wrote, "The superiority of her charms was felt and acknowledged by her companions, but without envy; for it was surpassed by the unassuming gentleness and winning kindness of her manners."

IDA YEATMAN RAINS (1837–1925). Private collection.

Granddaughter of West's brother, John Brown West; lived in Nashville. Andrews.

REFLECTION. Unlocated.

Exhibited at the British Institution in 1829.

JOHN RICHARDS (1787–1827), oil on canvas, 90.2 x 69.8 cm. (35½ x 27½ in.), circa 1818. Mississippi State Historical Museum, Jackson, Mississippi. *Illustrated on page 67.*

SARAH BUCKHOLTZ (MRS. JOHN) RICHARDS (1792–1886), oil on canvas, 90.2 x 69.8 cm. (35½ x 27½ in.), circa 1818. Mississippi State Historical Museum, Jackson, Mississippi. *Illustrated on page 69.*

THE SANCTUARY GAINED. Unlocated.

Exhibited at the Royal Academy in 1826.

KATRINA SCHUYLER. Unlocated.

Engraved by Joseph Andrews. FARL.

WILLIAM GILMORE SIMMS (1806–1870), oil on canvas, 76.2 x 63.5 cm. (30 x 25 in.), 1844. Private collection.

"This portrait was painted in 1844, when I was 38 years old, by William West the American (Kentucky) painter—an artist of great merit." Reproduced in William Gilmore Simms, *The Letters of William Gilmore Simms,* ed. Mary Simms Oliphant, frontispiece.

MARGARET SPEAR (MRS. SAMUEL) SMITH. GENERAL SAMUEL SMITH. Pair of portraits. After Gilbert Stuart. Oil on canvas, 76.2 x 63.5 cm. (30 x 25 in.), circa 1837–41. Maryland Historical Society, Baltimore.

Copied for sitters' daughter, Sidney Smith (Mrs. Edward) Patterson. CAP.

THOMAS CARTER SMITH, oil on canvas, 72.4 x 59 cm. (28½ x 23¼ in.), circa 1823. Private collection.

Painted in Italy, according to descendant. FARL.

ABRAHAM SPEARS, miniature painted circa 1805–8. Private collection.

Could be by John B. West. Whitley.

WILLIAM STEUART (1754–1838), oil on canvas, 76.2 x 63.5 cm. (30 x 25 in.), circa 1838. Private collection.

FARL.

RICHARD HENRY STUART (1808–1889), oil on canvas, 76.2 x 63.5 cm. (30 x 25 in.), circa 1839–41. Private collection.

FARL.

A STUDY. Unlocated.

Exhibited at the British Institution in 1829.

GOVERNOR THOMAS SWANN (1807–1883), oil on canvas, 76.2 x 63.5 cm. (30 x 25 in.), circa 1838–41. Private collection.

Tuckerman (*Book of the Artists*, p. 201) mentions having seen this work. JHP.

EMMA JANE WILSON (MRS. THOMAS UPSHUR) TEACKLE (1818–1861), oil on canvas, 76.2 x 63.5 cm. (30 x 25 in.), circa 1839–41. Private collection.

FARL, JHP.

THOMAS UPSHUR TEACKLE (1797–1863), oil on canvas, 76.2 x 63.5 cm. (30 x 25 in.), circa 1840. Private collection.

Attribution unlikely. West painted Mrs. Teackle, but this work looks more like that of O. T. Eddy. FARL, JHP.

ANNIE CAMPBELL GORDON (MRS. JOHN HANSON) THOMAS (1819–1886), oil on canvas, 76.2 x 63.5 cm. (30 x 25 in.), circa 1838. Baltimore Museum of Art, Maryland. *Illustrated on page 113.*

JOHN HANSON THOMAS (1813–1881), oil on canvas, 76.2 x 63.5 cm. (30 x 25 in.), circa 1838. Maryland Historical Society, Baltimore. *Illustrated on page 115.*

FARL, JHP, CAP.

MARTHA TRABUE (MRS. GEORGE) THOMPSON (1823–1901), oil on canvas, 76.2 x 60.9 cm. (30 x 24 in.), circa 1856. Private collection.

The subject was the niece of West's brother-in-law, Robert Woods, who married West's sister, Sarah. Last exhibited in "Tennessee Painting—The Past," Cheekwood, Nashville, Tennessee, 1960.

THE TOILET. Unlocated.

No additional information has come to light on this painting, exhibited at the British Institution in 1829, and again in 1837 when West's address is given as 15 Wigmore Street.

EDWARD JOHN TRELAWNY (1792–1881), oil on canvas, 69.8 x 55.2 cm. (27½ x 21¾ in.), 1829. Private collection. *Illustrated on page 89.*

EDWARD TURNER (1778–1860), oil on canvas, 74.9 x 61.6 cm. (29½ x 24¼ in.), circa 1848–50. Private collection. *Illustrated on page 133.*

ELIZA BAKER (MRS. EDWARD) TURNER (1789–1878), oil on canvas, 74.9 x 61.5 cm. (29½ x 24¼ in.), circa 1848–50. Private collection. *Illustrated on page 135.*

MARGARET PATTERSON (MRS. CHARLES COCKE) TURNER (1816–1873), oil on canvas, 76.2 x 63.5 cm. (30 x 25 in.), circa 1838. Maryland Historical Society, Baltimore. *Illustrated on page 117.*

FARL, JHP.

THE UNWILLING BRIDE. Unlocated.

Exhibited at the British Institution in 1837. Same work as *Adornment of the Bride?*

AARON VAIL. Unlocated.

Exhibited at the Royal Academy, 1833.

GEORGE WALTON (1786–1859), oil on canvas, 71.1 x 63.5 cm. (28 x 25 in.), circa 1815. Mobile Historical Preservation Society, Mobile, Alabama.

Attribution recorded by IAP unlikely. Reproduced in Colonial Dames, *Alabama Portraits*, p. 366.

SARAH MINGE WALKER (MRS. GEORGE) WALTON (1791–1861), oil on canvas, 73.7 x 60.9 cm. (29 x 24 in.). Mobile Historic Preservation Society, Mobile, Alabama.

Attribution by FARL unlikely. Reproduced in Colonial Dames, *Alabama Portraits*, p. 367.

GEORGE WASHINGTON (1732–1799). MARTHA DANDRIDGE CUSTIS (MRS. GEORGE) WASHINGTON (1731–1802). Pair of portraits. Oil on canvas, 76.2 x 63.5 cm. (30 x 25 in.), circa 1837–40.

Copies of Charles Willson Peale (George Washington) and John Wollaston (Martha Washington) portraits.

LEWIS WAY. Unlocated.

Washington Irving "found Mr. Way sitting for picture" (journal entry for April 16, 1825, published in his *Journals and Notebooks*, vol, 3, p. 476). The Reverend Lewis Way had an American Chapel in Paris, which was attended by West and Irving.

EDWARD WEST, JR. (1757–1827), oil on canvas, 73.7 x 58.4 cm. (29 x 23 in.), circa 1805. Nell Foster Waltz. *Illustrated on page 49.*

SARAH BROWN WEST (1761–1824). Private collection.

Andrews.

WILLIAM EDWARD WEST (1788–1857), self-portrait, oil on canvas, 76.2 x 60.9 cm. (30 x 24 in.), circa 1819. Private collection. *Illustrated on page 73.*

WILLIAM EDWARD WEST (1788–1857), self-portrait, oil on canvas, circa 1835. Unlocated. *Illustrated on page 31.*

Reproduced in Nellie Porterfield Dunn, "William Edward West," *Putnam's Magazine,* September 1907.

COLONEL JONATHAN WILLIAMS (1750–1815), oil on canvas, 205.6 x 157.3 cm. (81 x 58 in.), 1816. Unlocated.

Begun by West, finished by Sully; listed in Biddle and Fielding, *Sully,* as cat. no. 1984.

THOMAS WILSON (1777–1845), oil on canvas, 76.2 x 63.5 cm. (30 x 25 in.), 1839–41. Maryland Historical Society, Baltimore.

JHP.

MRS. ANNE THELLUSSON WINDHAM, oil on canvas, circa 1827–37. Private collection.

FARL, Witt.

LEVI WOODBURY (1798–1851), oil on canvas, 73.7 x 60.9 cm. (29 x 24 in.), 1839–41?. United States Supreme Court.

FARL.

WOODS. Private collection.

Male sitter. Andrews.

AGNES WOODS. Private collection.

Robert Woods's sister. Andrews.

JANE WEST WOODS (1785–1871). Private collection.

West's oldest sister; lived in Nashville. Andrews.

JOSEPH WOODS (1779–1859).

Married West's sister, Jane, in 1806; no issue. Andrews.

SARAH WEST (MRS. ROBERT) WOODS (1792–1879), oil on canvas, 58.4 x 71.1 cm. (23 x 28 in.) oval, circa 1855–57. Private collection.

West's sister, with whom he was living at the time of his death. Andrews.

WILLIAM HENRY DECOURCEY WRIGHT (1795–1864), oil on canvas, 76.2 x 63.5 cm. (30 x 25 in.), circa 1839–41. Private collection.

JHP, FARL.

MRS. WILLIAM HENRY DECOURCEY WRIGHT (1800–1864), oil on canvas, 76.2 x 63.5 cm. (30 x 25 in.), circa 1840. Private collection.

FARL, JHP.

LOUISE WURTZ. Unlocated.

Andrews.

MARY BYRD (MRS. SAMUEL GERRISH) WYMAN, oil on canvas, 75.6 x 62.2 cm. (29¾ x 24½ in.), circa 1837–41. Private collection.

FARL.

SAMUEL GERRISH WYMAN (1809–1883), oil on canvas, 1839–41. Private collection.

Unlikely attribution. FARL.

LAURA YEATMAN. Private collection.

Andrews.

BENJAMIN FARRAR YOUNG (1798–1860), oil on canvas, 78.7 x 63.5 cm. (31 x 25 in.), circa 1852. Private collection.

Reproduced in Colonial Dames, *Louisiana Portraits,* p. 274. Attribution questionable, and likely based on West's portrait of Young's sister, Elizabeth Henrietta Young.

ELIZABETH HENRIETTA YOUNG (1797–1870) AND ANNA ELIZABETH MERCER (1832–1851), oil on canvas, 124.4 x 99 cm. (49 x 39 in.), circa 1852. William Barrow Floyd. *Illustrated on page 137.*

CAP.

YOUNG LADY WITH VASE OF FLOWERS, oil on canvas, 91.4 x 73.7 cm. (36 x 29 in.), circa 1850. Private collection.

Sold at Sloan's auction house, Washington, D.C., in 1977, lot 1053. Attribution questionable but not refutable without examination. Vase of flowers in window is typical of West's post-Baltimore period.

Selected Bibliography

MANUSCRIPTS

NELLIE PORTERFIELD DUNN PAPERS. Alderman Library, University of Virginia, Charlottesville, Virginia.

GILMOR, JOHNSON AND PATTERSON family vertical files. Maryland Historical Society, Baltimore.

CHARLES HENRY HART PAPERS. Archives of American Art, Smithsonian Institution.

JOSEPH HOPKINSON PAPERS. Historical Society of Pennsylvania, Philadelphia.

J. HALL PLEASANTS files. Maryland Historical Society, Baltimore.

WILLIAM EDWARD WEST file. Frick Art Reference Library, New York, New York.

WILLIAM EDWARD WEST PAPERS. Archives of American Art, Smithsonian Institution, Washington, D. C.

WILLIAM EDWARD WEST PAPERS. Catalog of American Portraits, National Portrait Gallery, Smithsonian Institution, Washington, D. C.

UNPUBLISHED MATERIAL

ANDREWS, ELLA J., comp. "Descendants of Edward West, Inventor and Silversmith." Photocopy of typescript dated February 16, 1966. Collection of the author.

DUNN, NELLIE PORTERFIELD. "William Edward West." Tennessee State Library, Nashville. Unpublished draft of *Century Magazine* article containing complete typescripts of correspondence in family collections.

FLANARY, SARA LEWIS. "The Pre-European Career of William Edward West in New Orleans and Mississippi." Unpublished master's thesis, Cabell Library, Virginia Commonwealth University, Richmond.

WILLIAM PATTERSON will. Unpublished typescript. Maryland Historical Society, Baltimore.

SCHNEIDER, JAMES F. "Catalogue of Portraits in the Collection of the Baltimore City Court House." Archives of American Art, Smithsonian Institution, Washington, D. C.

BOOKS

Biographical and Historical Memoirs of Mississippi. Chicago, 1891.

COLLINS, LEWIS. *History of Kentucky.* Maysville, Kentucky, 1847.

DUNLAP, WILLIAM. *A History of the Rise and Progress of the Arts of Design in the United States.* 1834. Reprint. New York, 1969.

EATON, CLEMENT. *The Mind of the Old South.* Baton Rouge, 1967.

EVERETT, FRANK E., JR. *Brierfield Plantation Home of Jefferson Davis.* Hattiesburg, Mississippi, 1971.

FABIAN, MONROE H. *Mr. Sully, Portrait Painter: The Works of Thomas Sully (1783–1872)*. National Portrait Gallery, Smithsonian Institution. Washington, D. C., 1983.

HUDSON, ARTHUR PALMER. *Humor of the Old Deep South*. New York, 1936.

IRVING, WASHINGTON. *The Complete Works of Washington Irving in One Volume*. Paris, 1834. An edition contemporary with West's stay in Europe. Includes *Annette Delarbre* and *Pride of the Village*.

——. *Journals and Notebooks*. Volume 3, 1819–1827. Edited by Walter Reichart. Madison, Wisconsin, 1970.

——. *Letters*. Edited by Ralph M. Aderman, *et al.* Volume 2, 1823–1839; Volume 3, 1839–1845. Boston, 1979 and 1982.

JONES, ARTHUR F., AND BRUCE WEBER. *The Kentucky Painter from the Frontier Era to the Great War*. University of Kentucky Art Museum. Lexington, Kentucky, 1981.

KANE, HARNETT T. *Natchez on the Mississippi*. New York, 1947.

LOVELL, ERNEST J., JR., ed. *His Very Self and Voice: Collected Conversations of Lord Byron*. New York, 1954.

MARCHAND, LESLIE A. *Lord Byron: Selected Letters and Journals*. Cambridge, Massachusetts, 1982.

MOORE, THOMAS. *The Life, Letters, and Journals of Lord Byron*. London, 1920.

NATIONAL SOCIETY OF THE COLONIAL DAMES OF AMERICA IN THE STATE OF ALABAMA. *Alabama Portraits Prior to 1870*. Mobile, 1969.

NATIONAL SOCIETY OF THE COLONIAL DAMES OF AMERICA IN THE STATE OF GEORGIA. *Early Georgia Portraits 1715–1870*. Athens, Georgia, 1975.

NATIONAL SOCIETY OF THE COLONIAL DAMES OF AMERICA IN THE STATE OF LOUISIANA. *Louisiana Portraits*. New Orleans, 1975.

NATIONAL SOCIETY OF THE COLONIAL DAMES OF AMERICA IN THE STATE OF NORTH CAROLINA. *North Carolina Portrait Index. 1700–1860*. Chapel Hill, North Carolina, 1963.

RICHARDSON, EDGAR P. *The World of the Romantic Artist*. Detroit Institute of Arts. Detroit, 1944.

——. *Travelers in Arcadia, American Artists in Italy, 1830–1875*. Detroit Institute of Arts. Detroit, 1951.

ST. CLAIR, WILLIAM. *Trelawny, the Incurable Romancer*. London, 1977.

TRELAWNY, EDWARD JOHN. *Records of Shelley, Byron, and the Author*. 1878. Reprint. New York, 1968.

TUCKERMAN, HENRY T. *Book of the Artists, American Artist Life*. 1867. Reprint. New York, 1966.

WHITE, NEWMAN IVEY. *Shelley*. 2 vols. New York, 1940.

WHITLEY, EDNA TALBOTT. *Kentucky Ante-Bellum Portraiture*. The National Society of the Colonial Dames of America in the Commonwealth of Kentucky. Richmond, Virginia, 1956.

WILLIAMS, STANLEY T. *The Life of Washington Irving*. 2 vols. New York, 1935.

EXHIBITION
RECORDS

GRAVES, ALGERNON. *The Royal Academy of Art, A Complete Dictionary of Contributors and Their Work from Its Foundation in 1769 to 1904.* London, 1906.

——. *The British Institution 1806–1867*. Bath, England, 1969.

National Academy of Design Exhibition Record 1826–1860. New York, 1943.

RUTLEDGE, ANNA WELLS. *Cumulative Record of Exhibition Catalogs. The Pennsylvania Academy of the Fine Arts, The Society of Artists, 1800–1814, The Artists' Fund Society, 1835–1845*. Philadelphia, 1955.

ARTICLES

Dunn, Nellie Porterfield. "Unknown Pictures of Shelley." *Century Magazine,* October 1905, pp. 909 *ff.*

——. "An Artist of the Past: William Edward West and His Friends at Home and Abroad." *Putnam's Monthly,* September 1907, pp. 658 *ff.*

Flanary, Sara Lewis. "William Edward West in New Orleans and Mississippi," *Antiques* 124, no. 5 (November 1983): 1010 *ff.*

Floyd, William Barrow. "Portraits of Ante-Bellum Kentuckians," *Antiques* 105, no. 4 (April 1974): 808 *ff.*

Pennington, Estill Curtis. "Painting Lord Byron: An Account by William Edward West," *Archives of American Art Journal* 24, no. 2 (1984) pp. 16–21.

Ross, Marion Mulligan. "Story of West, Painter. . .," *Lexington* (Kentucky) *Leader,* May 1, 1921, Sunday supplement.

Index

The complete list of West's sitters is given alphabetically in the Checklist. Only those sitters also mentioned elsewhere in this book are included here.

Italicized page numbers refer to illustrations.

Designed by Gerard A. Valerio, Bookmark Studio

Composed in Baskerville Linotype by Brunographics, Baltimore, Maryland

Printed by The Collins Lithographing and Printing Company, Baltimore, Maryland on Potlatch Quintessence